"A grounded, depthful and beautifully hearticulated description of the dark night of the soul journey. The perfect book for anyone who is truly ready to confront and transform their shadow into the light at its source. Highly recommended!"

–**Jeff Brown**, author of *An Uncommon Bond* and *Grounded Spirituality*

"*The Dark Night of the Soul* portrays the hero's journey from the darkness of psychological desolation into the light of wholeness and integration. By tracing this little-explored landscape, Fiona Robertson provides a much-needed service: a map and a message of hope for anyone seeking a way forward in the midst of spiritual crisis."

-**Angelo John Lewis**, Director of the Diversity and Spirituality Network and author of *Notes for a New Age*

Published in the United Kingdom by Gawthorne Press
Unit 18519, PO Box 7169, Poole, BH15 9EL

Cover art by Stefan Armoneit
Cover design by Claire Crevey
Edited by Claire Crevey
Author photo by Tim Bryn Smith

ISBN 978-1-9164686-0-3

British Library Cataloguing-in-Publication Data
A catalogue record for this book is available from the British Library

The Dark Night of the Soul

A Journey from Absence to Presence

Fiona Robertson

Gawthorne Press

Contents

Foreword

As I write here in the spring of 2018, dependable political, sociocultural, psychological and ecological structures all around us are turning upside down. This is a time of great uncertainty. Many of us are questioning major paradigms, our most deeply held beliefs about ourselves and the world. In this incredible personal and collective breakdown, we are losing what we thought was real. As the structures of separation, rationalism and dualism collapse, we are waking up to an expanded sense of self very different from the self we were conditioned to believe in.

We are discovering a new paradigm of interconnectedness in lieu of remaining bound to a false self existing in isolation. More and more of us are experiencing self as multiplicity, self with porous boundaries, self beyond definition. Some of us experience these revelations through intense self-inquiry. As pure awareness, we come to know who we are cleanly, tacitly, untethered to the whims of thought, image and expectation.

Many of us are willing to investigate our inner worlds, to let go of who we thought we were and learn to be simply as we are. Through inner inquiry and spiritual breakdown, we get to know ourselves as we are for the first time since childhood. We return to who we were before our stories and wounds. It's not so much that we discover anything new about ourselves; it's more that we remember who we have always been, as interconnected beings in presence. We heal by reconnecting to the wholeness that has always been.

Because we are complex, the transformative journey of reclaiming wholeness takes many forms. As transpersonal researcher Stanislav Grof notes, sometimes our awakenings are gradual—we ease into remembering who we are, a spiritual emergence. For others, awakening crashes at the door in harsh, unyielding waves that nearly drown us. For some of us, this dying is the only way to finally live. This is known as a spiritual emergency, or as described in this critical work by Fiona Robertson, a dark night of the soul. It is a radical disillusionment, a life-transforming crucifixion of spirit.

In the following pages, we meet our *anam cara*, a collective of soul friends who share their stories, reminding us of who we are with no agenda of their own. Fiona's awakening stories gift us with rare insights into the journey of the dark night. We receive backstage access to the challenges of traversing the underworld. We are blessed to bear witness to the ongoing assimilation that arises on the flipside of the dark night. As Fiona notes, it is a journey of deepening without end.

I have heard it said that wisdom is a side effect of healing. Such wisdom is certainly evident in this book, revealing and reflecting Fiona's depths of healing. Her story interweaves and unites with the stories of others, all threads in the tapestry of our collective awakening. Together these stories support communion and affirmation for any reader, regardless of their experience in relation to awakening. This is not a fixed, static read but a multidimensional safe space; you are invited to crawl inside to experience awakening through a kaleidoscope of lenses and accounts. Further, this book is an opportunity to question the entire notion of awakening and a call to emerge more completely into our spiritual, social and ecological maturity through direct experience. Fiona's work reminds us there was never anything wrong with us to begin with, and that it's normal to grieve for the people we believed we were.

This book is right on time. Its messages were never more necessary and urgent—transformation is possible. The time to reclaim who we are is now. I'm honored to weave my thread into this tapestry of *anam cara*. We as your soul friends stand with you side by side as we welcome each other home in the simplicity of being.

As Presence,
Jen Peer Rich, MA, PhD (ABD)
Founder, Friends in Presence

Introduction

I have written this book for all those who are in the dark night of the soul, for those who have gone through it and for those who are curious about it. There seems to be a dearth of writings about the experience, which can make it feel lonelier or more frightening than it already is. Whilst this journey is ultimately made alone, I offer you my experience and insights along with those of the generous, open people I have had conversations with over the last few years. Our paths have crossed at various points in our dark night journeys—as friends and fellow travellers—and we have talked at length. I share some of their words here along with my own. We cannot give you a panacea or solution to the dark night, for neither exists, but perhaps our experiences will shed some light on yours. We have gone through the dark night and have all emerged bruised, humbled and unutterably grateful. Together we are your *anam cara,* your soul friend. Know that however intense it gets, you are not the only person to go through this. We too have traversed this paradoxical land, so foreign to those who have not encountered it, and we understand the language spoken here.

When the dark night came calling, it was because I had lost contact with myself in a fundamental way. It was a rebellion of the soul, a cry from the most essential part of my being. No longer able to countenance the half-life I was living, the deadened version of myself I had become, my soul ignited and dragged me, kicking and screaming, into the land of the living via the valley of the shadow of death. No longer willing to allow my continued absence from my own life, it demanded I become fully and honestly present. I was scared I would lose my life. I didn't imagine I would gain it.

The dark night of the soul was a descent into the heart of myself, a profound metamorphosis. It was a plunge into the shadow realms, into all I had unconsciously tried to suppress, deny or evade. It was the dissolution of all I thought I was. None of us would choose this willingly; I certainly did not. Yet there was a part of me that had longed for it, that had longed to be annihilated, to no longer have to be the character I had become. It was a journey of radical self-remembering and reconnection.

This descent into the realness of myself formed the prelude to an ongoing awakening process that continues to this day. In my view, the spiritual journey is not a matter of transcending or somehow overcoming our humanity, but of maturing into the depths of it, of realising and becoming who we really and uniquely are. There is no end to this unfolding; it does not conclude in some triumphant attainment or achievement, nor does it confer specialness in any shape or form. Such metamorphosis is unconditional; opening to life in the present inevitably entails opening to the unfelt pain of the past. Self-knowledge and even wisdom are forged in the embodying of pain in a way that cannot be taught. I have come to know myself in a way I could not have conceived possible prior to the dark night.

Whilst each of our dark nights is unique, our most personal and intimate experiences open the door to the universal. This is the archetypal journey described by mystics and sages down the centuries, an initiation into the mystery of life. Saint John of the Cross, the sixteenth-century poet and Christian mystic, was the first to use the phrase "dark night." One could equally call it a spiritual or existential crisis or emergency. We are becoming our authentic selves, and yet we are also coming to know ourselves as something beyond the individual. This is where spirit is made flesh. We touch the divinity in blood and bone. Spiritual teachings either crumble into dust or become our lived, embodied reality. This is the truth of awakening, far removed from the fantasy.

For most of us, the dark night of the soul is a deeply private experience. Few understand its intensity. Only those who have made the descent know the anguish and ecstasy that ensue. I found it difficult to speak about, particularly when I was in the midst of it. It transported me far beyond the known, beyond the limited horizons of my thinking, rational self. It stripped away all the trappings and roles I had become dependent upon. My life was altered in fundamental ways. It brought me to my knees, alternately begging for help and feeling the deepest gratitude.

Humankind seems to yearn for experiences of depth, awe and wonder. I was no exception. Since my teenage years, I had longed to connect with the numinous, to something greater than my small self. I had experimented fleetingly with psychoactive drugs, dabbled in meditation and made a more serious study of transpersonal psychology. During the dark night, I found myself immersed in this landscape with no choice but to abide there. At times it felt like being in a liminal space between worlds. I endured more suffering than I imagined possible. At times, I doubted my capacity to survive it. Yet from the start I knew that what I was experiencing was not an illness to be healed but a reclamation of my deepest being. The dark night is a ruthless taskmaster, an iconoclastic destroyer of preconceptions and assumptions. However tenaciously I clung to them, any ideas or beliefs I tried to hold on to in order to shore up my former sense of identity eventually crumbled. This is the territory of Kali, the Hindu goddess who brings destruction for the sake of radical liberation, and she is not polite.

During the dark night, I fell apart and was repeatedly broken open. A dynamic deepening into aliveness began, and it continues to this day, albeit in an evolving form. Even though I felt totally unprepared—for none of us can rehearse or prepare for this—I gradually realised there was a profound intelligence at work. Be assured the soul's call comes only when we are ready, despite our pleas to the contrary. As I have said, each of us experiences a unique version of the dark night. For some, it involves a complete upending of life, a cataclysmic falling apart. For others, it is less obviously dramatic; external life continues on relatively unruffled, but seismic changes are nevertheless taking place below the surface. Whatever the particular nature of your experience, know that it is every bit as valid as anything described in these pages.

A note on the structure of this book: each chapter focuses on a different aspect of the dark night. This may give the appearance of a linear experience with a beginning, middle and end. The reality is more complex. This journey does seem to have an arc, with distinct phases, yet it is also elliptical or rhythmical rather than strictly linear. I found myself coming back to the same places repeatedly, experiencing them anew each time. Likewise, the language of the soul is poetic rather than conceptual, mythic rather than psychiatric. It embraces paradox and may seem contradictory to the analytical mind. Here, words are potent yet fluid and interchangeable. Many have no precise meaning, or our understanding of their meaning changes and deepens over time. I came to know these words far beyond my intellectual understanding of them, their resonance touching me in unexpected, unfathomable ways. Conversely, words that had once seemed significant lost any import at all. Not everything you read here may make logical sense, but hopefully the words will impart the dark night's raw, unfiltered, visceral flavour.

Throughout the book, I use a variety of interchangeable terms to describe the part of us that alchemically alters during the dark night: the acquired self, false self, adapted self, mask, persona or ego. None of these words are used pejoratively. This part of our being is a feat of ingenuity, a creation of necessary inventiveness. Much as it may sometimes behave badly or feel flawed, it deserves a paean all to itself.

There is no elegant way to go through the dark night. I stumbled, struggled, fought, cursed, prayed, wept, surrendered, raged, accepted, resisted and denied, all in equal measure. There were times when I could not find relief, when no options seemed to remain. But there were also unexpected, impossible-to-predict moments of love, understanding and awe. Moments when grace infused me and I became more alive than I had ever been. Moments when I marvelled at life's astounding mysteries. Moments when I bathed in the essence of myself. It was in those moments that I recognised the true gifts of the dark night, gifts I am still receiving to this day. I hope you come to taste them for yourself.

Chapter One: The Crash

I had supposed an epic, life-changing event would herald my transformation, an epiphany set against a scene of stunning natural beauty, a defining, significance-drenched moment. I had imagined that when the time came, I would be transported from the drab mundane to the exalted sublime, to a paradise of bliss or calm, to the end of all suffering. I had read about enlightenment and longed for the *coup de grâce* that would deliver me from myself. My soul was not supposed to be roused by a curt letter from the city council.

I was doing well, up until that morning. I finally seemed to have the life that had been so elusive for such a long time. No longer carrying around the familiar feeling that I was not living up to my early promise, I had become the person I wanted to be. For several years, I had been building the material infrastructure of my life. At last, I was successful in my career and had received national acknowledgment for my work. My child was thriving, and I had done up my house. I had even met a professional man with an important job title, a radical departure from my previous boyfriends.

Inwardly too, I felt more settled and less neurotic. All the years of therapy and self-development seemed to have paid off. My childhood pain far behind me, I was no longer the one who didn't fit in, the ugly duckling. Not only feeling good, I was looking good, too—fit and slim. Perhaps a little too slim, a good friend warned.

And yet, in quiet moments, I had a palpable feeling that none of this was really the point. An indefinable something seemed to be pulling me down and back. Despite its insistence, I ignored it. Now was not the time. I had a new lover to keep up with, a clinic to manage, clients to treat, a fitness schedule to maintain. Brittleness crept in, and there were moments when I felt hollow, as if there were nothing substantial beneath my surface. I became controlling, harsher, more convinced of my rightness. It had taken so many years and so much effort to reach this destination, I wasn't about to let it all go now.

That April morning, the letter I received from the city council thwarted my plan to sell my house and move in with my partner. Four years or so earlier, I had received a housing improvement grant on condition that I reside in the house for at least five years. If I moved sooner, the penalty would cost thousands of pounds. Having hoped the council would relent given the condition expired in a few months' time, initially I fumed. Then spontaneously, inexplicably, I began to laugh. I saw the futility of my attempts to control my circumstances. It felt momentarily wonderful to give up a struggle I hadn't even been aware I was engaged in. It was as if I had found a part of myself I hadn't known was missing. I suddenly realised that I didn't need to fight any more, didn't need to try any more. I could be me, without the need for changes, improvements, alterations, embellishments. I had tried so hard for so long. I had believed that if I didn't do it, make it or say it, it wouldn't be done, made or said. I had believed that I had to earn my place, affection or support by grafting, by constantly putting other people's needs first, and by being less—or more—than myself. In that moment, I didn't know which way the journey would lead, but I felt less attached, freer, more able to let things be. Finally, I could do without forcing. I could act without pushing. I could rest without guilt. I could lie and be supported, sleep and be held. A few words from Verse Thirty-Two of the *Tao Te Ching* sprang to mind:

> One must know when to stop.
> Knowing when to stop averts trouble.[1]

I knew change was on the horizon, as yet unseen. I knew something profound had happened, but I imagined life would carry on just as before. A strong sense came to me that it was all going to be alright, whatever it was. I carried on with my day, walking across the park to the clinic, feeling lighter and freer than I had in a long time. The trouble was I didn't know when or how to stop, so Lao Tzu's words went unheeded even as I quoted them. I had no idea what was just around the corner.

Later that week, I dreamt of being in my house and realising there had been a crash. Prompted by its vividness, I recorded the dream in my journal:

> *I go into the kitchen and a chunk of the ceiling has fallen down. In the bathroom, the floor has collapsed at one end. I go through the house, calling for my mother. I tell her what the problem is, and we talk to a woman from the*

---

[1] *Tao Te Ching* by Lao Tzu. Translated by Gia-Fu Feng and Jane English.

insurance company, who advises us about underpinning, doing a proper job so it won't happen again.[2]

Life seemed to return to normal for two weeks. Then the crash I had dreamt of happened. I hit the wall at a hundred miles an hour, or that's what it felt like. My life began falling apart at lightning speed, as did I. I had tried hard to keep it all together when really, I'd known this was coming. I had courted it, this crash; I had danced with it, even as I resisted it. I had wanted to steer the ship into safe harbour before I jumped overboard. Even in those first few days, I knew what the problem was: I had lost touch with my soul. I'd become disconnected. I was in deep crisis.

Virtually overnight, I lost my ability to function in the outside world. Previously efficient at work, a good communicator and confident with clients, I could barely stand, let alone interact. Waves of anxiety and fear engulfed me. Tears sprang without warning. Within a week, I had withdrawn from the clinic, leaving my business partner to navigate her way through the funding shortfall we faced. The dark night—or the crash as I then called it—had begun.

The first few weeks passed in a blur of tears, sleepless nights, anxiety, dreams and terror. I would wake at two or three in the morning in intense anguish, hot and sweating. I went to bed every night believing I wouldn't wake up in the morning. I was convinced that what I was experiencing wasn't survivable. I felt ill, my head buzzing. I cried a lot. At

---

[2] All quotes in italics are from my journals.

times I'd read, write or try to meditate. I spent a lot of time lying down. I knew I needed time to be with the process as it unfolded. I imagined it would take two or three months to find my way back. I imagined normal functioning would eventually be restored, and I would return to my life as I knew it. I couldn't have been more wrong.

The crash takes a different form for each of us. An event may precipitate it, or it may arrive with little forewarning and no obvious cause. For me, as I've described, it was shockingly sudden. For some people, it comes as a gradual wearing down of the spirit, unobservable to onlookers. Either way, it becomes apparent that however hard we try, we can no longer maintain the persona, the part of us that has been trying to live up to demands and expectations from both within and without. In all my busyness, I had lost sight of myself and my deeper needs. Like millions of other public-sector workers, the hardest part of my job was liaising with funding bodies and trying to make my clients' experiences—including torture, homelessness, drug addiction, abuse and self-harm—fit a tick-box culture. I had taken on work until it buried me. I couldn't walk away and say, "This is what I need for me." I couldn't take any more. I couldn't feel for myself any more. I had no real idea what I needed. Even when I did, I thought I couldn't have it.

I don't think it was coincidental that the dark night began once I came close to becoming the person I imagined I should be. While trying to reach my ego ideal, I had tended not to question the fantasy version of myself to which I was aspiring. This image of the perfect me was so deeply ingrained that I had taken it to be a valid, matter-of-fact destination, my personal and achievable El Dorado.[3] The drive to reach this destination was fuelled by a rampant superego with a long list of "shoulds," and I did not question their authority or validity. Various marketplaces encourage and exploit such striving, including sectors of the self-help, spiritual and personal development industries. We are sold the idea that we need to work hard on ourselves, that we can only become what we strive to be by taking up this practice or subscribing to that belief system. But once I crashed, I realised I had been barking up the wrong tree. Becoming the person I had believed I should be did not bring about the happiness or contentment I had imagined it would, simply because it wasn't who I really was. In fact, becoming that person meant repressing or denying large parts of who I actually was. Just before his dark night began, my friend Per[4] also reached a point in his life when everything seemed to have come together:

> At least externally, I had everything: a wife, a beautiful house, a nice situation. All the things you need. A nice car. The things you're supposed to have to be successful. Just before I got the chronic fatigue, I was thinking that all the pieces are in place in terms of having a successful life, in terms of social standing.

As my life and health fell apart, I could no longer perpetuate the fiction that I could become an *uber*-version of myself if only I tried hard enough.

---

[3] In his novel *Candide*, Voltaire (François-Marie Arouet) named his ideal land El Dorado.
[4] I recorded a series of interviews with others who have gone through the dark night; all quotes are from the transcripts.

It was overwhelmingly disappointing to face up to the impossibility of becoming what I imagined I should be. The movement to become *that* rather than being *this* ran deep. It felt as if I had failed dismally and completely. Yet relief was also palpable; the endless striving had been exhausting and soul-crushing.

How is it that we can end up so disconnected from our true selves? I believe it is partly because as children, those influencing us could not, for whatever reasons, consistently allow us to be who we were. Those responsible for us could not countenance or accept certain aspects of our being—character traits, feelings or physical attributes—so we learnt to suppress or hide those parts that were deemed to be not okay. We adapted our natural temperaments to become what we believed we needed to be in order to survive in the circumstances. We became a facsimile, a fake version of our real selves. Little wonder many of us have an underlying sense of being an imposter who will eventually be unmasked. We also unconsciously mourn for the loss of our real self, hidden beneath the swathes of adaptation and conditioning.

My mask depended on mechanisms of suppression, avoidance and defence. As the dark night began, these began to break down. I could no longer hold the unwanted or rejected parts of myself at bay. Cracks appeared in the structure; the dam burst. My house, built on the insubstantial sands of the false self, began to collapse. Everything I had attempted not to feel emerged. It felt like a catastrophic loss of control. My persona ran around trying to keep it all up, out and in. To let go of the delusion of control was a huge challenge.

Once events exposed the illusory nature of the control I thought I had over life, it was shocking to realise I could no longer control my experience either. The illusion of control had allowed my persona to operate in the world and keep itself intact, warding off basic, existential fears most of the time. Without this illusion, the persona was disintegrating. Whilst it was initially a relief to see the insubstantial nature of the control I thought I had, it soon became terrifying. I was terrified of losing control, of the void, the huge nothingness I sensed beyond. I thought that if I stopped, I would be annihilated. I had been trying to keep the mask I believed myself to be alive and pushed myself to the edge in the process.

However hard I tried, I could not control or manage the deluge of emotions, sensations, memories and thoughts that poured forth once the dam burst. This was an affront to my ego; I prided myself on self-control and self-containment. The crash happened despite all the therapeutic and developmental work I had done since my late twenties. The idea of becoming a better version of myself was swiftly swept away. In retrospect, I doubt any spiritual practice or therapeutic modality can stop the dark night once it is on its way because its very purpose is to move us beyond any notion of improving, changing or managing what is here.

Sometimes the dark night comes after some kind of awakening experience or a period of meditation or spiritual practice. The idea that such practices are always benign, that mindfulness and meditation only lead to positive feeling states, is erroneous and misleading. These practices can crack the shell of the adapted self, exposing all that lies beneath. If one has engaged in them in order to feel better or calmer, or to move towards the ideal self-image, it can be a rude awakening indeed. Other times, the spiritual journey begins with the dark night.

Either way, even in the moments when we feel as if we have no choice, we know that deep down we have chosen this. The soul has been calling, and we can no longer ignore its cries. Prior to the dark night, I was dimly aware of a longing to uncover the truth of my being, a call to awakening, although I did not use that term at the time. The old adage to be careful what you wish for seems apt here. Per talks about his dangerous prayer:

> For me, there was a lighter phase of the dark night, like a gradual onset that lasted for several years. I really had a sense I was reaching the tail end. And that's when I had the awakening, and suddenly it got twenty times worse. After maybe two or three years in the heavier phase, I did start to feel much better, and then I made another of those dangerous prayers, where I said, "Show me what's left." Within a week, I had the intense terror come up for nine months.[5]

Having wished for this, I could not hold back the tide however hard I tried. This was a time of reckoning. All I had ever evaded, avoided or distracted myself from came to the surface. Shockingly raw fragments of the past

---

[5] Per, in conversation.

came spontaneously into consciousness. The pain of a lifetime was laid bare, and me along with it. There was no other way to unravel the self that I had become because the unfelt pain of the past was its very fabric. There was no other way but down and through. Rather than transcending the painful past, I descended right into it. Andrew describes this succinctly:

> A swami once told me that when you start digging into the real nature of things, the past comes up for reconciliation—and that's essentially what the dark night of the soul is, in my opinion. You open the cupboard to clean out your room and pull out all the junk, and the room gets messier before it gets cleaner. As it's piling up, things get worse. It's all junk from the past, and it overshadows your awareness. It's this heavy muck that you're attached to because it's your story and it's your stuff, and I don't think there's any easy way around it.[6]

Though the feelings were often very intense, sometimes their release felt cleansing or purifying. In my experience, such deep and near-continual catharsis is rare outside of the dark night. It took a long while to learn how to be with the ebb and flow as things came up. In covering similar terrain over and over again, everything that emerged felt simultaneously new and familiar. The process felt interminable, and yet there was also a subtle sense of movement or shift. I gradually became familiar with the tides.

I frequently doubted that any transformation was occurring because there was no external or visible change. I would look for signs that

---

[6] Andrew, in conversation.

I was getting better according to my old yardsticks of how I should be and was profoundly disappointed to see I wasn't improving according to those criteria. Despite the disappointment and a strong sense of having failed, I also knew there was no going back. As the dark night continued, trust in the process began to emerge, even in the midst of despair and hopelessness. In this subterranean world, the tectonic changes taking place did not become apparent for a long time.

The crash, shocking and painful though it was, felt necessary. I had to be brought to a halt, removed from the confines of my previous existence with its routines, responsibilities and roles, in order to make the descent. As with Per, illness brought me to a near-complete standstill. I was menopausal and had an underactive thyroid. At various points, I also thought I was going through a nervous breakdown or burnout. And while there was validity to all these diagnoses, I knew they were only part of the picture. The dark night was so much more than a collection of physical or mental symptoms, although it included these. In truth, part of me wanted to be ill. I wanted the pressure and the having-to-do to stop. I wanted to go within. I wanted the gift of time and quiet.

As well as coming to a halt, I could not return to the presumed or actual security of my previous existence because large parts of it were no longer there. The clinic closed down, so my job was gone. The soul's call issues forth in unavoidable ways and leaves us with little room for manoeuvre. Life ensures that we cannot ignore this invitation. In one of our dark night conversations, Sutra Ray described how she experienced this in a particularly dramatic form:

> I received a really clear message that it was time to leave where I was living, this lovely little cottage. I heard that message so clearly, and yet I thought, "Well, maybe not yet." Then I was out of town for a few days and got a phone call from the owner of the house: "Sorry, an eighty-foot fir tree has completely crushed the cottage. Good job you weren't here." I didn't have any choice after that. It was a big experience, this tree cutting my cottage in half.[7]

The unique circumstances necessary for the unfolding of each dark night occur in uncanny ways. Some people experience almost no change in their external lives, continuing to function outwardly as they previously did. Others may find themselves feeling compelled to make changes—entering relationships, moving town or country, leaving a long-held job or partnership—seemingly against their better judgement. It is as if life creates the crucible required for our distillation. Adversity is often the catalyst that brings us out of our habitual lives, our business-as-usual mode. Andrew says:

> Nature organises things. It organises for people to be in situations where there's no way out. It's like life would conspire to put me in these impossible situations where I'd be absolutely screwed. And I'd look at it and think, "The only way I could possibly be in this terrible situation is if there's an invisible hand that put me here." By noticing the perfection of the mess, it's like, "Oh, there's a

---

[7] Sutra Ray, in conversation.

thread I can pull here." It was like a grand conspiracy. You've just got to hold on to your seat.[8]

This phase of the dark night challenged every level of my being. I struggled to deal with my everyday life and responsibilities. Even a trip to the local supermarket felt like climbing Everest on some days. I struggled to eat. My sleep was affected—insomnia seems to be a hallmark symptom of the dark night. The lack of sleep further eroded my ability to function. I swung between trying to keep the structure of my life intact and being willing to let everything fall apart. I had to strip everything back to the basics and go to ground, only doing whatever absolutely had to be done. My life became tiny and circumscribed.

I needed to work out which activities or practices felt nourishing and supportive and which did not. My findings ran counter to my expectations. What I had previously found useful lost all benefit, and I was drawn to things I had once dismissed. Meditation became so uncomfortable as to be tortuous, while walking around the streets and the local parks sometimes felt relieving. There are no prescriptions or recipes for the dark night; it cannot be problem-solved. Relying on my intellect or ideas about what I should do didn't work, and neither did taking other people's advice or suggestions. I had to feel my way in the dark, gradually learning to trust my instincts.

---

[8] Andrew, in conversation.

Sometimes I could not find comfort or support anywhere—nothing I tried was of any use. For a long time, I believed this was my fault. I would fall back into desperately trying to change or improve my experience, to no avail. Later, I realised this incessant trying was a way of abandoning myself. In the absence of any other option, I had no choice but to be present. I was taken to the brink and beyond, time and time again.

As I crashed, I was called to pay close attention, to notice the direction in which I was being drawn moment by moment, step by step. There could be no grand plan or strategy, for this was the undoing of such thinking. My focus changed day to day. For one six-week stretch, I was drawn to watching the daily television show of a spiritual medium. I had never been remotely interested in such things beforehand and have never watched anything like that since, but during that period, it felt imperative to do so. The things I found myself doing were sometimes totally at odds with how I had previously seen myself. All I could do was follow the scent as best I could.

In this phase, I thrashed and flailed about, desperately trying to work out what to do, how to be or where to go. I cast about for solutions, intently trying to work out what would stop the crash from happening. This activity was not entirely in vain because sometimes I discovered things that were helpful or soothing, at least in the short-term. However, all the running from pillar to post left me exhausted. When I did pause, the part of me that was still trying to control the process was frantic, noisy and terrified. In moments when all else failed, I would lie down and breathe as best I could. I had a deep yearning for simplicity. I longed to live in a cottage by the sea, under the silent care of a wise, older woman. That particular desire remained unfulfilled, but I began to find slivers of silence and stillness in my everyday life in the city: a walk in the park, moments of music, quiet times in the dead of night.

Crashing is hard on both mind and body. I reeled from the shock of it for some time. Without doubt, being thrust out of my former life felt like a catastrophe rather than the start of a spiritual journey. Yet I gradually began to experience moments of relief that I no longer had to defend myself against what was really here. I didn't have to try in vain to contain it all any more. The pressure had been so great that I had been bound to fail. I hit the wall, and the dam burst. This was not a defeat, I later realised, but a cessation.

Chapter Two: Falling

It cannot be overstated just how deeply the dark night takes us into felt experience, the sheer viscerality of our being. Here, where reason holds no sway, the logical self is utterly unable to manage or deal with what is happening. Whatever our accomplishments in the outer world and however intelligent we are, we cannot think or engineer our way out of this.

As I descended into this realm, I felt as if I were teetering on a gangplank, about to fall to my death. I could not go back the way I had come because my former life—and my former self—no longer existed. The only option seemed to be an unavoidable plummet over the vertiginously high edge, a horrendous, catastrophic smash that I couldn't possibly survive. It felt as if I must hold on with every fibre of my being to avoid being annihilated or obliterated. And in a way, this was true. The persona I had become and tried to perfect over the years was indeed falling apart. Because I didn't fully know that I existed beyond this false persona, I naturally feared my imminent demise. I clung desperately to the sheer cliff face, fingers bleeding, attempting to claw my way back to the supposed safety of the mountain top. The impossibility of simultaneously holding on and letting go created unbearable tension throughout my system. I felt trapped between equal and opposite forces. I could not yet fall, but holding on was not a viable option either.

The ideas, beliefs and concepts I had lived by began to unravel. Without their apparent solidity and stability, life felt tenuous. I fell into the unknown. This is the terrain of the dark night, unnavigable by reason. The unknown—that which the mind does not or cannot know—appears terrifying. We see images of black holes, endless voids, unbounded space. In our conversations, Per, Rachel and Anja each described their experiences of this falling into the unknown.

> During those months when I had the dread and terror, as soon as I put my head down on the pillow and turned off the light, it was as if I were falling in space, as if there were nothing there. There was no reference point, nothing. That was pretty scary. After a while, I got quite used to it.[9]

> I felt panicky, absolutely exhausted and completely overwhelmed. I've got such a strong holding-it-together piece, but underneath it was all falling apart, it really was all falling apart. I had no ground. I just kept falling. I felt like I was literally falling. I was falling down this abyss. I would call people, trying to grasp onto something, but there was nothing anybody could do. That night you came over I really thought I was going to fall off the world, fall off the universe and disappear forever into a complete black hole.[10]

> I remember this experience like a falling. It's really a falling into nothing. You have no idea what is happening, you just feel there's something really going on. There was also a time of doubt. Is this

---

[9] Per, in conversation.
[10] Rachel, in conversation.

my fantasy? But there is something going on. Like a falling, a falling apart of what you think you are. I think this is the deepest fear.[11]

The much-vaunted spiritual cliché that we should let go is of no help here. If we could simply let go, we would. But when it feels as if our very survival is at stake, it is totally counterintuitive to acquiesce. Our whole being braces against the fall. The nervous system, sensing danger, keeps us alive in the only way it knows how. Holding on is exhausting, but it is even more exhausting and painful to try to let go when we can't. We can only be patient, however frustrating that may be and however desperate we may become.

Despite my bracing against the fall, gravity eventually did its work. I was bone-deep exhausted and could no longer hold on, despite my desperation to do so. Dull and numb, tired and defensive, I no longer had the fight to resist. It was not so much a letting go as a giving up, the ultimate defeat of the adapted self. It felt like utter failure. To this day, I don't know exactly how or when I landed. I found my grip loosening, first a finger or two, then both hands. I began to see that the holding on had been an attempt to protect the soft, vulnerable flesh of my real self. A shred of gentleness or kindness began to infiltrate the harshness and terror of the descent. Willing now to go all the way, I began to lower myself down. I survived, despite my expectations of calamity. Upon landing, the downward plunge became a falling apart, a falling into or even a falling away. Old patterns and conditioning began to unravel as my persona shed

---

[11] Anja, in conversation.

its protective snakeskin. I found myself in an in-between state, a kind of limbo. The old had crumbled and gone and the new was not yet sensed. I felt adrift, without any bearings as to who and where I was.

A part of me had longed to jump. My soul, desperate to break out of the restrictive carapace of the adapted self, with all its caveats and conditions, had lured me to this edge. I had climbed to the highest spot I could find and pulled the ladder up after me. I wanted to ensure there was no going back. Falling was terrifying, but it was also a relief. Constant vigilance had been required to ensure my authentic self did not seep through into consciousness. It had taken so much effort to maintain the barricades. I had expended so much energy holding on. As time went by, my adapted self lightened as I sloughed off what I no longer required. This way of being in the world simply didn't work any more. I felt it dissolving, falling away.

This falling apart rarely conforms to our notion of how things should be. It is not neat, predictable or orderly. Some of us cannot keep it from infiltrating every aspect of our lives. It does not wait for an invitation, as Rachel describes:

> Literally, the falling apart would just happen anywhere. It was indiscriminate. I'd be in public places, in the supermarket, at work. It just became part of my life. I was so blown and broken open, I couldn't hold any of it. It had to come out. It was time for it to come out. It knew no boundaries. It had no social etiquette. It continued to unravel. It brought all that childhood stuff that had been holding me back to the surface. It had to literally break me

open. It was deeply humiliating and humbling, very, very humbling.[12]

My beliefs about what it meant to be me were coming undone. I discovered that even the positive facets of my adapted persona took a great deal of effort to maintain. The idea that I needed to be clever was one of the first beliefs to fall away. I had held fast to this belief in my cleverness since early childhood because it was one of the few ways I had received praise. I was naturally a clever girl, as my school reports attested, but as I got older, my need to be clever—and to be seen to be clever—became ever-more pronounced. I made concerted efforts to come top of the class in each subject. Throughout adulthood, I had prided myself on cleverness and intellectual acuity, considering myself well-informed, knowledgeable and articulate. Yet in the early months of the dark night, a spontaneous shift happened, accompanied by a huge sense of relief:

I don't have to know anything. I don't have to try to understand quantum physics or mathematics. I don't have to know what's going on in Mexico or Turkmenistan or even the bottom of the garden. I don't have to know the Prime Minister's name or who won this year's Booker Prize. I don't have to know the names of birds or trees or flowers or fish. I don't need to know people's names or job titles, ages or places of birth. I don't have to know why I do the things I do or why I sometimes suffer. I don't need to be clever any more. Maybe I'll work in a cake shop. Maybe I'll be a gardener's assistant and spend the day digging and watering and listening to birds. Maybe I'll walk other people's dogs. Just no more brain work. No more figuring things out or trying to be knowledgeable. I'm joyous at the thought of not being clever any more.

Without the burden of needing to be clever, I could now enjoy knowledge for its own sake. This spontaneous falling away of old conditioning is a central part of the dark night experience. Sometimes it is incredibly painful, at other times joyous or even amusing. There is such a paradox at work here. As what we thought we were falls away, we become so much more ourselves. This is a fall from the heady heights and lofty ideals of the adapted self down to the earthiness of the real self, from what we supposed we should be to what we actually are. As the binds of my beliefs and conditioning loosened, I discovered it was not only pain that had been suppressed. Other aspects of my natural temperament—joy, silliness, humour, fun, creativity, power—began to emerge as the persona lost its dominance. I began to feel like myself again. Sutra Ray describes:

> It's a falling away rather than an adding on. Most of our lives we've spent adding on, creating more identity and meaning. What remains when conditioning falls away? That's the fun part. We spend so much time trying to follow the norm, to not stand out, to be a good person, to not make waves, all those things, and we really miss who we are. Who is this person, really? I think that's where the maturity is, to finally become yourself... You can't be yourself until everything else falls away.[13]

---

[13] Sutra Ray, in conversation.

This phase of the dark night was all-consuming. It was particularly challenging to function when I was experiencing tremendous anxiety, grief, shame and other intense emotions. I didn't really function most of the time. I did my best to shop, cook, clean and look after my teenage son. I tried to keep my falling apart to daytime hours when everyone else was out of the house. Some days I cried for hours. I lay awake for long periods in the night. There were times when I seriously feared for my sanity. I was terrified of falling down the rabbit hole and never coming back, of descending into madness.

After a while, I understood there was no right or wrong way to traverse the dark night. Finding my way through was a matter of constant experimentation. Only I could really know what I needed, despite the recommendations or exhortations of others. Psychotherapeutic interventions, healing modalities of various kinds, meditation, exercise—I tried them all with varying results. Regardless of what I did or how much I tried to change its course, the dark night had its own pace and rhythm. It would not be undercut, hurried or prematurely ended.

When the sense of falling was intense, I would feel the solidity of doors, floors, walls and the ground beneath me. When I could not trust anything or anyone else, I could depend on the physical world. I could lean against the wall and slide down to the realness of the floor supporting me. In those moments, I didn't have to hold myself up. Likewise, being on grass or around trees, walking by the canal or river gave me a comforting sense of the physicality of the world.

Even when I felt entirely dysfunctional, there would be something I still loved, something I could still do. As everything fell apart, I noticed what remained. When the waters recede, the shipwrecks of our real selves become visible. Whether it is movement, prayer, some kind of artistic or creative endeavour, gardening, or meditation, these can be our practices. For me, it was writing. For Rachel, it was dancing:

> The only things I could do were get on my yoga mat, sit in the sea, or dance. I could dance for six hours straight, yet I could barely walk to the shops. What it really showed me is where the true energy is in me, what is really my true, authentic self. The things that are genuinely in alignment with my true self remained, and they were the only things that remained. Everything that essentially wasn't me fell apart and away. The things that were essentially me stood out like beacons and became my signposts. That time is an opportunity to see those threads of who we truly are. Because they don't die. They don't fall apart. If anything, they get more illuminated.[14]

Reassurance from someone who understands the dark night experience might provide a crumb of relief. The majority of us go through the dark night on our own, so words of reassurance may be hard to come by. I found comfort in a handful of books, poems and songs. Luann says:

> Even though some people were supportive, I had never seen anybody go through this. It would have been so helpful at the beginning for someone to say, "You are going through a dark night

---

[14] Rachel, in conversation.

of the soul. You're going to think it's going to be endless. You're going to want to die to get out of the pain. But this is age-old. This is what the spiritual masters have talked about. And you will come out of it better." Even though I had the inner knowing of that, I questioned it.[15]

Falling apart is both simple and hard. When falling is the only option, resisting it is terrifying and occasionally hilarious. I had so many beliefs about letting go, about what I should and should not do, that I complicated the process. I thought there were things I had to keep, archive and catalogue, memories and hurts to resolve, an arduous journey to make. But there came a time when I found myself willing to fall. I didn't know how to fall, but that was okay. The falling happened regardless, in its own time. I did not need to make the falling happen, nor could I. As I fell, I discovered that trying not to fall was much harder and more painful than the falling itself. Despite myself, I encountered moments of humour amidst the terror and panic, moments when I tripped and fell headlong however hard I tried to stay upright.

I discovered this was not a project at which I could succeed or fail. Letting myself fall was such a relief. I discovered the grace in being unable to put myself back together. Rather than the fall from grace it initially appeared to be, the dark night was a fall into grace. I wanted to be so broken that repair was impossible. I wanted to let the walls around me fall. As I was writing one day, I heard the message, "You're here to receive, to

---

[15] Luann, in conversation.

take what is given, to surrender. Absolutely everything is given. All the pain comes from not knowing that you just don't know. Such is grace." Not yet fully knowing what that meant, I nevertheless took heart.

Chapter Three: In the Underworld

As I entered the dark night, it took a long while to adjust to the *yin* underworld. When, like Persephone,[16] I disappeared below ground for long periods of time, the *yang* world of activity and doing no longer made sense. In any case, I found myself incapable of participating in it. While my Demeter self raged above ground, I knew that Hades would have his due, however much I railed against my incarceration. Eventually, I learnt to spend time in both realms, becoming equally familiar with above and below.

In the underworld, my vision seemed altered. Nothing looked as it had before, despite its familiarity. At first, I found myself groping around helplessly, unable to work out what to do, where to go or how to be. I had no option but to take one small step at a time, and sometimes couldn't even do that. And yet, within the first few weeks, insights started to surface. Every few days, some moment of illumination or understanding would come. One day, I saw that I had always been in opposition; I had taken the stance of the other, the against, the anti. Seeing this brought a softening, a sense of simply being without explanation, reaction or apology. Such realisations made the underworld slightly more bearable.

---

[16] In Greek mythology, Persephone was the daughter of Zeus and Demeter. She was abducted by Hades, god of the underworld, and became his queen. Her grief-stricken mother, not knowing where she was, desperately searched the earth for her. Persephone was said to rise above ground in spring and descend again during the winter months.

As I descended into the shadow realm, my mind and body panicked. I was entering unknown territory. My adapted self had done its utmost to keep me away from this forbidden region. In this place resided the parts of myself I had left, neglected, suppressed or ignored. They didn't fit my image of who I should be. Most of them had been too painful for me to harbour. Even as my soul demanded I traverse this terrain, I fought back with every fibre of my being. I wanted to return to the known and familiar. Instead, I entered the underworld, coming ever closer to the Minotaur's lair.[17] These were strange, dark days, filled with tears, palpitations, desperate searching and occasional understanding. I tried hard to get away. I tried to get rid of *it*. I hated it and tried to avoid, evade, ignore or overrule it. One day, I stopped long enough to wonder—what was it?

Fear of the dark, or what may be in the dark, is common. In dominant culture, light has come to connote positivity, goodness and rightness, consigning dark to the opposite pole of negativity, badness and wrongness. The dark is demonised. Nowhere is this more obvious than in attitudes to skin colour. Yet as the *yin-yang* symbol so elegantly illustrates, dark and light embody the two equal, interdependent primal forces that give rise to the universe. Each is inherent within the other. Neither can be itself without the other. Much as we cannot see in the dark, we can equally be blinded by the light. The glare of light can be harshly defining, bleaching

---

[17] In Greek mythology, the Minotaur was a half-bull, half-human creature living in a dark labyrinth.

and demanding. Either way, our vision is obscured. As nature unerringly reminds us, we cannot have day without night, summer without winter, light without dark. Darkness, in all its manifestations, is natural, and we are not separate from nature.

In my view, much of modern spirituality has lost its balance. The cult of lightness and so-called positivity is endemic. Those emotions characterised as negative—terror, fury, fear, shame, angst, guilt, outrage, grief, resentment, sadness, horror, jealousy, envy, rage, sorrow, anger, hatred and so on—are repressed, denied and often pathologized, regardless of what may have prompted them and however fitting a reaction they may be to the circumstances in which we find ourselves. We are expected to adjust our naturally sane selves to an insane society and to display only those emotions that are culturally sanctioned. The same happens within family systems and communities, of course. Those who are unable or unwilling to conform to this norm may even be scapegoated or punished. Hardly surprisingly, we end up feeling bad for having such feelings, not least because we get the message that their presence indicates some deficiency on our part. When we find ourselves subsumed by them, we assume there is something deeply wrong with us, rather than questioning the biases inherent in our culture.

While it was initially frightening to be in this nether world, I began to notice the security and comfort of the dark. I could hide a while in the darkness, undefined and indistinguishable from everything around me. I found myself drawn to sitting in small, dark spaces. Especially when I was very distressed, I would crawl into the wardrobe, shut the door, and sit hunched like a small child or animal. It was the only place that felt safe— nothing coming in, very little light or sound, no intrusions. All outlines and separateness gone, the darkness felt gentle and forgiving. It was as if my body needed some respite from the overstimulation of the light world, from having to *be* somebody.

In the dark, I encountered repressed or denied aspects of myself. I discovered a multiplicity of parts, a parade of sub-personalities whose existence I had barely surmised, let alone admitted. Some of them felt like separate entities, such was the degree of their suppression. The qualities and feelings I had distanced myself from came home to roost. This incremental re-owning of my shadow happened spontaneously and awakened the possibility of moving beyond the straitjacket of shoulds and oughts that had constricted me. For someone who considered herself empathetic and caring, it was unflattering and humbling to discover parts of myself that were totally at odds with my self-image as a good person. While painful, this process was often deeply energising. I no longer had to contain, nor could I hold back, the powerful currents within. There were times when I felt hard, aggressive, bleak, strong and empty, times when I despised my normal, caring self. I had had enough of caring in order to prove that I was "nice." What did it matter, in the greater scheme of things, whether I lived or died? Who gave a shit? I didn't care.

Any aspect of the real self, any trait or feeling, may end up in the shadow. One day, I realised I had disowned my strength. I had espoused meekness and weakness to shelter me from my own strength. Rather than countenance my own strength, I had taken comfort in buckling in the face of others. My persona found safety in collapse because as a child, that had seemed the safer option:

> *I didn't want to be strong. I thought you had to be a bitch to be strong, so I sided with the weak. I've been scared to admit my own strength. I hid my strength so well it was even hidden from me. I couldn't bear to see it, so I sabotaged it at every turn. All those times I denied my strength, played small, played weak. Yet there is a ground here so firm, so unshakeable.*

The shadow is not merely an individual phenomenon. The long and intertwined shadows cast by patriarchy, colonialism, imperialism and capitalism include the full array of oppression, prejudice and violence of all kinds, including environmental degradation, war and rape. Whatever the particular intersection at which we personally stand, we all live under these shadows, whether we benefit from them, are disenfranchised by them, or both. During the dark night, we are called to withdraw from this matrix. Sophie had a high-profile media career for twenty years, yet she came to a point when she could no longer participate:

> I don't think it's just personal stuff we haven't faced, or a turning away from ourselves. I think it's something much deeper. I think every single thing about this planet, the way we live, is totally wrong. I was absolutely forced to stop living in this rapacious, hungry, career-driven way, looking on the outside for happiness. If society is a woven carpet, we are being forced to pull our thread out of it. The strands of your life have to be unpicked from the

whole of society. And the more people who pull out their threads, the more it collapses. We're not upholding it any more by buying into all our stories. When that is let go of, there's more of a melting into the whole somehow.[18]

As individuals, groups and nations, we project onto others, creating enemies and scapegoats. Rather than remove the beam from our own eye, we attempt to remove the speck from the eyes of others. An us-and-them mentality pervades our interactions. Left unexamined, it runs amok. In the dark night, we are called to face the repercussions of our projections. As we encounter our personal shadows, we may also encounter the collective shadow, as Per describes:

> In the beginning, I had all these archetypal images come up. One night, for hours, I had these pictures of all the evil characters in mythology from all over the world parading in front of me. I became them for a moment, and then they moved on and I became the next one. It went on for hours. There was this owning of the shadow in the archetypal sense.[19]

Throughout the dark night, we also meet the pain of having been scapegoated or projected upon, of having been in the familial or societal shadow. Many of us have borne the brunt of others' hostility, aggression, fear or unconsciousness. The pain of being the "other" in our families, communities or the wider world can be immense and intractable. Again,

---

[18] Sophie, in conversation.
[19] Per, in conversation.

we feel both individual and collective pain depending on our gender, race, sexuality, class, creed or disability. Whatever we have denied will emerge, be it rage, outrage, grief, shame, strength, pride or feelings of any other hue. Any attempt to undercut the fierceness of these feelings with platitudes or rationales is a violation. We can no longer normalise pain and degradation, even if we believe our sensitivities and feelings make us wrong, or if other people wrong us for having them. We might even come to see that what we thought was wrong with us is actually what is right with us.

Here in the underworld, an encounter with the shadow of death is inevitable. Death is the inescapable certainty around which we dance, the riddle at the heart of existence, the great leveller. None of us truly knows what will happen when we die. Contemplation of death is generally considered morbid and discouraged, especially in death-phobic cultures like mine. The bereaved, expected to come to terms with their loss unreasonably quickly so as not to remind others of the reality of death, often grieve silently. In my late twenties I went through a period of profound fear of death after the sudden passing of a friend. Having lessened in the intervening years, this terror was powerfully resurrected during the dark night.

My adapted self did not believe it could survive the feelings that were breaking through to consciousness. It felt it was in mortal danger once its defences had been breached. The dark night did indeed spell the end of my persona as I had known it. This version of myself was facing its own demise, regardless of all its manoeuvres. I felt like I was dying, even though I knew I was probably not physiologically at risk. Not surprisingly, this felt terrifying. There was no getting out of the process once it was underway. I was convinced that the pain would kill me. My persona seemed to have held me together—to acknowledge or release it must be the end of me. I had tried to engineer my life so I would not have to feel all this. Despite my terror of death, I also connected with a deep and incomprehensible ambivalence about being here, as if I had doubted I wanted to be born.

A deep longing or desire for death can also come up during the dark night. It can feel as if death is the only way out of the anguish. A powerful self-hatred can arise, the superego's hatred of the real self. It seems it would rather we died than accept ourselves as *that*, as all it has tried not to be. The shadow of death is persistently and powerfully present, and we can become consumed with the prospect of death. This facing of our mortality can shake us to the core. When we only know ourselves as the adapted self, it naturally feels like our actual, physical death is imminent in these circumstances.

Little by little, however, we become aware that we are more than this limited persona. We come to realise the person we think of as "me" is unquantifiable and unfathomable, a mysterious being who cannot be easily defined or categorised. Even though there are times we doubt we will survive beyond the next moment, we find ourselves waking up each day, taking one step after another, still here. What is dying is not the real self, but the part of us that developed to protect our authentic selves. What is dying is not who we really are. While we mourn its loss, we become more alive in its absence. We find ourselves surrendering to the process, willing to nail ourselves to this cross, as Stefano describes:

> There was more and more surrender and giving up, more malleability and just wanting to die to it all, not caring. I went through this whole psychological death.[20]

This willingness to die is unlike being terrified of death or suicidal. It is a readiness to die to ourselves, to all that is false within us, to return home. It is a relinquishing of control, the deepest kind of letting go. It reminds us of both our immensity and our glorious insignificance. It comes with tears and sometimes laughter. It wakes us up to the very fact of our existence. We were created. We were given life. It is such a wonder that we exist. How could we forget that? How could we take it for granted? Yet we do, for much of our lives.

My relationship to the concept of death gradually changed during the dark night and continues to change. Insights into both physical death and the death of the persona arose spontaneously. I cannot cling to such insights as a bulwark against the mysteries of death and my disbelief and grief when someone dies. The realisations themselves live and die. There are no fixed points in this territory, no places to land.

---

[20] Stefano, in conversation.

Beneath my fear of death lay the terror that I would never really feel alive again. Until the dark night began, I had no idea I was in a state of numbness and disconnection, let alone that I was terrified. Since my late teens, I had at various times attempted to rekindle my aliveness via sex, relationships, drugs and food, but such attempts had only spiralled me even more deeply into this half-deadened state. During the dark night my aliveness was slowly and painfully excavated. Each time I grieved for a lost, hurt or stolen fragment of myself, I reconnected a little more. Each time I admitted what had been scattered, scorned or neglected, I became truer to myself. This process of self-retrieval carries on to this day. It gives rise to an aliveness I had not felt since I was a young child, before the adaptation and denial began in earnest.

With much in my life and my adapted self dying, the dark night inevitably entailed loss. I lost much of what I had held fast to: the work I had loved so much, my health as I had known it, my income, confidence and some friendships. I grieved for each of these losses. And while I had longed to reconnect with my real self, I also mourned the loss of my persona, my way of being in the world up until this point. I was proud of her and what she'd achieved. She had flowered, blossomed and shone. I missed my work and was really lost without it. I had enjoyed recognition and acclaim. It was difficult to face the fact that all this was gone. I mourned the loss of hope that I could or would ever become my ideal self.

Relinquishing both our fantasies and major components of our actual lives is both painful and humbling, as Per describes:

During those dark night years, I lost my marriage, my house, my job, a lot of friends, my health… Almost everything that was important to me was gone. My identity, obviously—I had a strong identity of being active, self-sufficient, and productive. I ended up living with my parents again. It was hard in terms of my identity. I didn't feel proud of living back at home.[21]

Despite my losses, all that was most real within me remained. I was laid bare, without the trappings upon which I had previously depended for safety, security or a sense of self. I grieved and discovered love in the depths of the grief. I mourned and discovered the endless capacity for compassion within my heart, a capacity inherent in each of us and accessible when we touch these depths.

There are no rules on how to be in the underworld. A movement arises within, and it knows the way. There is nothing to do, despite our own or others' expectations. The pain may feel unsurvivable. It can feel as if we *are* the mess of pain we feel. The anguish and torment may seem like they will go on forever. We can become so enmeshed in and blinded by our beliefs about what is happening that we lose sight of reality. The truth is we will survive, and there is a way to navigate the underworld even if it is not yet evident. For the time being, we may need to find a port in the storm, something to anchor us or give us respite. In particular, those of us who feel suicidal need to reach out for help and do whatever it takes to

---

[21] Per, in conversation.

keep ourselves alive, trusting that one day we will touch our magnificence, the miraculousness of our being.

When the intensity of my inner experience consumed me, I tended to overlook physical reality. I sometimes became fixated on my thoughts and feelings to the exclusion of everything around me. Over time, I began to find comfort and reprieve in the stability of the material world. I longed for the actual: the cushion, floor, pen. The actual is solid and dependable. That's why shrines, mosques, temples, cathedrals and synagogues were built. There is depth in the very fabric of life, in stone, metal, cotton and water, in wood, bread and wool. I wanted the honesty of the actual. I wanted to work with my hands. All else felt dishonest. I wanted to be simple. I wanted to be, simply. The actual revealed its divinity:

> *I didn't know what I was. And you always here, steady, unchanging, patient, holding me, holding it all, containing every drop. Trees being trees, cars being cars, the sky being the sky. I am contained, container and containing. Such exquisite, delicate tenderness.*

My sojourn in the underworld revealed life's mysteries. Here, I remembered what I had forgotten and became myself again. Being in the darkness initiated me into a deep sense of aliveness. I became more willing to immerse myself in the wholeness of life, in the immensity of my being. I began to live more wildly and unapologetically than ever before. After all, the point is not to come through life unscathed. We are here to scar, to heal, and to discover the wholeness in both. Tempered in the forge of pain, we soften if, and only if, we let life in. Don't misunderstand like I did: you are not here to make a good job of this. Love is not borne out of perfection. We are all unbelievably precious. Countless unique creatures, billions and billions of unique lives all with their sublime nature, each one beyond miraculous, including you. At this time in history, one hundred and seven billion people have lived on this planet. What a privilege it is to be alive.

Chapter Four: Unravelling

I stopped loving me, except for a tiny spark buried deep, deep down.

In my experience, awakening is not a matter of transcending the ego. The notion of getting rid of the ego, even if such a thing were possible or desirable, seems to hold attraction only for the ego itself. Instead, the dark night process brings every aspect of the self structure to consciousness in order to be heard and transmuted. It is a process of distillation, an unravelling or disentangling of the false from the real. The dark night takes us far beyond any ideas or notions we have about the ego, awakening or spirituality as a whole. In fact, it often feels like the opposite of awakening, as if we could not be further from what we imagine awakening to be.

We are all familiar with the word "ego," yet its exact meaning remains elusive. We think of it as the sense of self, the voice in our heads, the "I." In some spiritual teachings, it is cast as a villain, a homogeneous and separate entity, an impediment to awakening we must subdue or overcome. In other teachings, it is merely an illusion, a ghost in the machine with no basis in reality. During the dark night, I came to know the ego and its various functions and layers in intimate detail. I discovered its intricately interwoven strands. What I found did not, in the main, conform to what I had been taught. I came to a deep love and appreciation for all it does for me.

The persona does its utmost to stop its own unravelling. At the start of the dark night, I could barely imagine who or what I was if not the ego. I had identified with it for so long that it was profoundly disorientating when it began to fall apart. I desperately cast about for the next version of me, unable to stop and rest and see that she was already here. My true being felt so insubstantial, contrary to expectations, and fleeting. Yet she was also deeply familiar. She was the young girl who had loved flower fairy books. She was the teenager who had gone beachcombing and written a poem about British mercenaries in Angola. She was the twenty-year-old who had picked up a bass guitar one new year's night.

Amongst other functions, the adapted self creates a protective distance between the inner self and its experiences. It filters what comes in and goes out, trying to protect us from potential, perceived or actual harm. It represses the mess and chaos within and attempts to control the flow of life. It ensures that the world sees an appropriate version of "me", in alignment with external criteria and conditioning. It adheres to the script it has been given as closely as it can. The superego—the critical, judgemental part of the ego—attempts to keep us in line with its diktats. The amount of protective distance required depends upon circumstances. Those who grew up in nurturing, loving homes or communities generally have less pronounced protection or control mechanisms. Those who have consistently experienced adverse, traumatic or unnurturing situations tend to develop more hyperalert, finely tuned defences. There is wisdom in our biology. Such defences form because they are needed.

The persona's defensive or protective aspect is not simply a matter of thought and mind; it is interwoven into the very fabric of our bodies. We experience it in a variety of somatic forms, including sensations, emotions, and subtle senses or energies. We may feel it as a contracted hardness or tightness, as if there are barriers, shields, armour or other defensive structures within us. At some point in the past, these defences were necessary for our survival. Our nervous systems created the best protection mechanisms they could to cope with the circumstances at the time. We cannot dismiss or dismantle them at will.

Several years prior to the dark night, I had become acutely aware of my defences. The story of the princess in the tower strongly resonated. The orphaned princess, stranded in the many-walled castle her protective father built for her before he died, is cut off from life until a wise knight appears. He understands that her walls will not be demolished by force but rather by love, understanding and gentle questioning. During the dark night, the true extent of Fortress Fiona revealed itself. I felt isolated, disconnected and shut down. Determined not to open, my fortress was trying to defend me. I had hardened at some point in the distant past because I thought I would be destroyed if I didn't. I was terrified to release the hardness because I still believed I would be annihilated if I let my guard down. I also recognised a withholding, withdrawal, and sense of superiority in my defended stance. These defences belied the reality of the soft flesh beneath. Maintaining the fortress was utterly exhausting. My body and mind could no longer keep it together. It became untenable to hold the structure in place. As it crumbled, I came face-to-face with the pain that had given rise to it in the first place. As the defences fell, the reasons why they had been created were exposed.

I began to realise how stultifying all the defending and controlling had been. It was as if I had been wearing a suffocating or restrictive, albeit protective, mask. I also began to realise just how much pain lay beneath it. Part of the mask's function was to protect me from having to feel this pain, and to ensure that no one else could see it. As the pain began to break through to the surface, the mask cracked.

> *I'm so tired. I'm so ashamed. That's why I've kept the walls up. That's why I've pushed people away, kept them at a distance, so that they don't see inside: the emptiness, the mess, the dirt, the barrenness, the disarray. If I really let anyone in, they'll see the truth.*

We tend to imagine that if people really saw the mess behind the mask, they would reject, exclude or condemn us. I thought that whatever was behind my defences was so awful, bad, toxic or shameful that exposing it would leave me alone, unloved, shunned or even dead. No wonder I was scared to be my authentic self. I pretended to be okay when things were not okay, yet I simultaneously yearned for an intimacy deep enough to breach the walls. I longed for another to see and know me. More than anything, I longed to reconnect with the deeply buried sense of my real self.

The ego or persona deems much of our inner experience unacceptable. As children, we were overtly or implicitly taught that certain feelings or behaviours were off-limits. Others might have shamed, punished, bullied or abused us for our emotions, self-expression, creativity, sexuality, gender, ethnicity or physical attributes. We might have learnt to feel unworthy, unlovable, insufficient or flawed. Parents might have neglected us, oblivious to our needs or too self-absorbed to pay us attention.

The persona or ego inevitably perceives itself as deficient in some way, whatever our personal history. If we were to be exposed, its worst fears would come true. Its whole function is to prevent such exposure, keeping buried what has been buried. It uses all kinds of behaviour to that end. My superego was perfectionist and controlling. It constantly monitored my intake and output, with food and everything else. It dispensed endless judgement and criticism. It endlessly checked, corrected, restricted and denied. It was scared, anti-life, fixed, rigid and cut off from my heart. I paid a high price for the protection, security and certainty it appeared to give me. I adapted and survived, but it cost me my aliveness.

Needless to say, I fought hard to maintain my self-image for as long as I could so as to avoid an unmasking. I tried to prove myself right in order to keep my mask intact. I wanted others to validate my version of me and felt threatened, hurt or offended when their validation was not forthcoming. I tried to make the storylines of my personal narrative work. My persona desperately wanted to achieve success and avoid what it perceived as failure. As the dark night wore on, I saw such successes were pyrrhic. I might claim rightness, but at what cost? What if I was wrong?

What if I stopped trying to prove everything I had set such store by? What if I resigned from this approval project, no longer labouring to get others to say yes to what I thought I was? What if nothing or nobody confirmed my version of me?

As well as being defensive and sometimes on the offensive, the persona is also on a mission to improve or perfect itself according to its own specifications, as I described earlier. It believes that if it can reach its goal, it will finally make up for or get what it perceives it lacks, be it safety, love, worth, value or significance. Fuelled by a sense of scarcity or inadequacy, the relentless pressure to better ourselves—which our cultures and economies feed—is difficult to avoid, particularly for those of us with a perfectionist personality. Perfection, by definition, is a state we can rarely reach. When we inevitably fall short of it, we interpret this failure as further evidence of our own deficiency.

It was not until I deeply questioned the very basis of my ego ideal—and the wider social narratives that fuelled it—that I realised there was another way to live. Having been a perfectionist from a young age, I had found many ways to make my life hard and to be hard on myself. I thought life was hard because I wasn't making enough effort. I thought other people's lives were better than mine because they were trying harder than me. I felt like a failure because I was exhausted. I stayed exhausted because I didn't know how to give up trying so hard. I thought life had to be difficult, that relationships had to be difficult, that all of it, including me, was difficult. I thought that was just how it was. For a long time, I didn't realise there was an option to see differently.

> *No wonder life has been hard. Such huge, unrealistic expectations and pressures so much of the time. To be a perfect girl, a clever girl, a thin girl, a popular girl, a good girl, a right girl. I turned my back on me. I tried to not be like me. Me was such a painful place to be. And I just wasn't perfect enough. It's been so long since I've been me. I've missed my me-ness. It's been so exhausting being her, such weight of expectation, perfection. I don't want to be her any more. I've longed to be me but haven't known how to stop being her. Now I'm finding the path of least resistance.*

The persona develops through interactions with its environment. Parents, caregivers, family, friends, educators and the wider community and society shape its beliefs and reactions, as do pivotal childhood events. It comes up with the best strategies it can to avoid harm and to get its needs met. It modifies the *prima materia* of our being to fit the circumstances in which we live. Even though some of its strategies may end up being deeply dysfunctional, they begin as an attempt to survive both physically and psychologically.

The self adapts in ingenious ways, according to its circumstances and its nature. From early childhood onwards, we may try to emulate those around us for their approval or to stop them from harming us. We might try to prove we are not what other people say we are, especially when they are critical or accusatory. We may deny our own needs in the belief that denying ourselves and trying to please or serve others will somehow result in them giving us the love and care we need. We may sacrifice parts of ourselves in the belief that doing so will secure our own or others' survival. We inevitably introject or internalise beliefs and emotions from those around us, incorporating their feelings and behaviour into ourselves. We model our relationship with ourselves on our earliest relationships—we tend to do to ourselves what has been done to us, even when we try not to. Until we become aware of them, these patterns run unconsciously, shaping our relationships and how we interact or withdraw.

As the dark night continued, I began to sense the utter futility of my persona's strategies. I did not have the energy to maintain them. I could no longer manage, avoid or deny the pain that was there regardless of all my strategising. I witnessed the whole movement of trying to be liked, trying to get love. I had tried hard to make people like me and had felt hurt and confused when they didn't. The thing was, I didn't like me either. I had tried to find the place where I fitted. I had tried hard to do the right thing by everybody. But none of it had worked. No solutions had materialised. All hopes of betterment were gone. The collapse of these failed strategies brought both grief and relief. Initially, it felt like a monumental defeat, as if I were everything I had feared I might be and had tried not to be. I had to face the original pain of not getting what I needed or wanted. Likewise, to stop attempting to please or mould myself to others' expectations—or what I believed their expectations were—was frightening, painful and liberating.

All these years of trying not to be my real self had taken their toll. I had toned myself down, dulled myself and disowned parts that seemed to have brought me pain or shame. But by shutting these parts out, I had lost their wisdom and aliveness. It was as if my true development, my soul development, was arrested until I reconnected with them. The good news was that despite my fears, the original self, before self-criticism, self-judgement and self-censorship, was still here. I had abandoned her, covered her up, and lost my faith and nerve. I had stayed small, hiding. Nonetheless, she remained.

As I exhumed her, I found myself caught in the crossfire between my adapted self and the parts of me I had repressed or denied. All of them needed their due. The task was excruciatingly difficult at times. A multitude of feelings surfaced as the inner status quo broke down. Each aspect of my persona made itself known in no uncertain terms, including my scathing, exacting superego. That part of me had interacted with people, looked after me, talked when I didn't know how, kept me in line, kept me motivated, and blocked out the pain before I could really face it. She had been trying to be what she thought a grownup was. She couldn't do all that without despising my weakness, pain, and failures. Her scalding hatred and shame burned:

> *I hate you, I really hate you. I'm glad you've suffered. So fucking pathetic and stupid. All those ridiculous relationships. No wonder no one liked you. How can you have been taken in like that? Where's your fight? Sitting around, thinking that being good is all it takes. You betrayed me so many countless times. I hate you for settling, so often, for the most meagre of crumbs.*

In addition to expressing her contempt and disgust for my flaws and weaknesses, Superego Fiona revealed her exasperation and exhaustion. She had tried hard, based on familial and cultural blueprints, to protect me from harm and ensure that I followed internalised rules. She tried to keep me together, make me the best person I could be, and protect me. She had been afraid for me. She believed, as did I, that without her, nothing would get done. She felt responsible for my survival. She was terrified to let go in case I died without her. Despite all her reproaches, she loved me:

> *I've been so angry with you for being so stupid sometimes. I love you, but I'm resentful of your sweetness and prettiness, your gentleness and kindness, your dreaminess and imagination. I've been so exhausted having to look after you. Sometimes I just wanted you to leave me alone and stop needing me.*
>
> *You kept insisting on pushing yourself and getting into bad, painful, hurtful situations. You completely freaked me out. God, I've been so frantic, panicked, worried. How could you do all that? Really, a trail of disasters, catastrophes. On what possible planet can any of those have been a good idea? You were such a sweet, beautiful little girl, with so much promise. I tried. I really, really tried. I tried so hard to keep you safe, to keep you on track, and you wouldn't listen. You thought you weren't enough. You thought you were second best. You thought you were fucked up, flawed, mad, not okay, damaged. You truly believed that deep down, you were the problem.*

Likewise, I began to hear from the parts of me that had been subjected to the superego's attacks and criticisms all these years. It was painful to be at the mercy of this scolding inner voice, not least because I believed it was telling the truth and I was everything it said I was. I hadn't known there was an alternative to believing it. Having spent years either trying to obey my superego's admonitions or disprove its damning assertions, I was shocked to realise just how hostile my inner environment had become. I was hard, harsh and hateful towards myself. I had introjected criticisms as a child and then perpetuated them *ad infinitum*. Paradoxically, it was when I truly acknowledged what I had unwittingly done to myself that I began to feel immense gratitude for all the superego had done for me. I came to realise it was not the enemy within.

> *I suddenly realise … so much judgement, so much criticism, so much pressure. I'm so sorry that I've put you under so much pressure. How could I ever feel there was something wrong with me? How could I do that to myself? I forgive me for treating me so badly, so unkindly. It's me I've been defending against. It's me that didn't feel safe. It's me that I've wanted to leave.*
>
> *Oh, you've been trying so hard to look after me, so anxious, so concerned, so vigilant. Thank you so much. Thank you so, so much. I know you've given absolutely everything. I am humbled. You cared for me so much. You care for me so much that you give me all that. And I've been trying to get rid of you, subdue you. I'm sorry. I didn't understand.*

As I journeyed through the layers of the adapted self towards the core of my being, I discovered a deep, primal "no." As children we inevitably experienced some degree of powerlessness, helplessness or hopelessness, particularly if we endured any kind of abuse, neglect or trauma. When our limits were not respected or our boundaries violated, perhaps we could not say an external no. We may not have known how to say no, or it may have been unsafe or dangerous to do so. Whatever our childhood situation, we expressed our truths as best we could.

The unheard or unacknowledged no remains within, even after many decades. The adapted self formed, in part, as an attempt to say no to what was overwhelming or unacceptable to us. As it unravels, we meet this no time and time again. *No, I don't want this. No, this should not be happening. No, this isn't right or fair. I can and I will resist this.* Realizing the extent of the no and feeling the bodily energy of it gives us a profound sense of ourselves and our boundaries, which may have been eroded over the years. We may have learnt to disrespect and dishonour our limits. As we connect with the no, we become more loyal to ourselves.

Depending on the degree of physical or psychological damage we have sustained, the no can feel impenetrable, as if our bodies contain a cement or stone wall. Our nervous systems do their best to prevent further harm. If we were traumatised as babies or young children, the whole world may feel threatening or unsafe. It can feel as if we are saying no to life itself. To push the no or suggest it should not be here compounds our trauma or injury. When we were little, the no tried to save us. It is part of our survival mechanism. As we approach it, it is bound to be suspicious of our intentions towards it. It has come to mistrust everything but itself, often for good reason.

I realised I was perfectly aligned with the no. Something in me was saying no to everything. *No, over my dead body.* The no believed bad things would happen if I said yes. Someone I loved would be hurt, or I would lose someone. As the no begins to express itself, our bodies may shake, sob or tremble. As Candace describes, it can feel overwhelming:

It's about a no. It's the opposite of "Thy will be done." No, thy fucking will not be done. My will be done. There are times when I can't feel that no all the way through because it's huge. I can feel it ten per cent and then I need to go for a walk.[22]

Spiritual or religious teachings that exhort acceptance or forgiveness may overlook the immense and crucial importance of hearing, validating and honouring our no. It is not a mistake or an enemy to overcome. There is deep intelligence within it. It is a reliable guide to our needs and how they might be met. At some time in our lives, our survival depended on it, psychically and sometimes physically, yet the smooth functioning of the adapted self depends on us disconnecting from it. It feels as if we cannot afford to listen to or act on our no. We need to put others' needs first, live up to our ideal self-image, or both. Our no feels taboo, and we fear its implications. I spent many years second-guessing and overriding my instinctive reactions, the no held in my body. I ignored or dismissed it and acted in spite of it, particularly in relationships. I paid a heavy price for doing so.

During the dark night, it is nigh on impossible to ignore it any longer. It becomes a piercing scream, a profound clench in the body. However we try to circumvent it, it demands our attention. Saying yes to the no allows it to fully express itself. When we listen to it, we discover what it is saying no to. It says no to pain, degradation and abuse. It says no to violence, neglect and unjust criticism. It says no to not being seen, heard,

---

[22] Candace, in conversation.

understood or valued. Meeting our no allows us to sort the wheat from the chaff, to clearly see what we accept and reject. It helps us learn how to recognise and express our deepest needs.

The no is not only personal. Not only have we lost touch with ourselves, we have become dangerously disconnected from each other and the earth itself. We know, deep down, how dysfunctional our societies are, and we can no longer participate. As we emerge from denial about our own pain, we cannot help but rage and grieve for our people, our countries and our world. We intuit there is another way to live, though we might feel clueless as to how to bring it about. We may long to live in a place where the only currencies are attention, presence, love and beauty, where nothing is bought or sold, where everything remains uncommodified. All we can do is feel our no to the core of our being and let it take us where it will, be it into activism, retreat or both.

Our no contains anger, rage and fury. Rage for the times we were treated badly or unfairly. Fury at the continuing pain and suffering inflicted on us, people we love, and humanity at large. Anger at our inability to effect change. Why would we not rage against those who have perpetrated against us? So often vilified, this anger is catalysing. It throws off our shackles, speaks up for us, breaks our silence, brings us out of enforced passivity. Its radical, cleansing energy cleaves through hokum. It brings into sharp relief all that needs to be excised.

We might be afraid to feel our fury, particularly if we endured the uncontrolled rage of adults when we were young. We may believe that if we feel our anger, we will become like those people who inflicted such pain and terror on us. It took me a while to edge towards my anger, but when it came, it was roaring. I raged, cursed and swore, pen nearly scoring through paper: "You bastards. You lying, hypocritical bastards." I would shut the door and scream into the duvet, punching pillows. "That's not fair" was the refrain ringing down the years. Hatred and outrage, fury and anger, these were the bricks with which my walls were built. Everything I had come to believe, about myself and everything else, was lies.

No, no, no, no, no, no. I tried to play by your rules, tried to fit, and you just broke me. How could you? I became in response to your attacks. I became aggressive and defensive, and I rejected and put up walls because you attacked me. I fucking turned myself inside out for you. I was in relation and reaction to you. You tied me in knots and then told me I was a tortured soul. All that politeness, polite civilised society. But politeness stops us speaking out, it stops us from telling it how it is. All that politeness when I wanted to scream, shout and cry. No more Ms. Polite Girl.

Alongside the no and its accompanying rage, we discover our deepest wounding, which commonly includes abandonment, loss and rejection. The adapted self formed in response to and around this wounding. During the dark night, the raw energy of the initial wounding arises insistently. Despite our resistance to meeting it, we eventually have no choice. It often has the energy of a frightened, ashamed, grief-stricken child. It is the part of us that has never been met, seen or loved. We have spent our lives trying to avoid it. It needs to be met as tenderly as possible, to be seen, heard, acknowledged. This wound, which has unconsciously run our lives for so long, seems to permeate our nervous systems. Candace describes her experience of meeting it:

> Every time I try to define it in a nice little package, words don't really … It can be all sorts of things—anger, grief, fear. It's that core firing, saying "Not okay, not okay, not okay." I meet it and say, "You're okay." I don't think there's any other way. It's a balance of having love, compassion and tenderness and the strength to say "Walk with me. We're going to look around and notice that everything is okay."[23]

When I first encountered my wounding, it felt as if I would never get over it. It appeared to be an endless, gaping wound, so vast, deep, and hopeless that all my attempts to make it better seemed pathetic and forlorn. In my childhood there had been no choice but to abandon and deny it, so all these years it had lain unacknowledged and untended. I met it in myriad ways. Once my defences were worn down, I was too exhausted and demoralised to do anything but give over to it. I made space for it and listened as it yielded its story. I came to understand I was allowed to be upset, that it was not wrong or shameful, and that there was no need to stop it. There were times when I could not face the wound, when I would do anything I could to shut it out. It remained insistent. The dark night had come because this wounding now demanded my undivided attention. Occasionally I would connect with a bountiful love and compassion for

---

[23] Candace, in conversation.

myself. I had been vulnerable and sensitive when the wounding had happened, as all young children are. I realised my innocence.

There were times when I longed for the wounding to be healed, when I bought into the notion of healing because the pain was so raw, intense, and excruciating to feel. Yet even the idea of healing came to feel like a violation of my wounding, an intimation that it was somehow wrong or flawed. After many years of personal and professional investment in the concept of healing, I found myself unequivocally saying no to it. My persona had enthusiastically bought into healing because it was desperately trying not to feel this pain. Now I didn't want healing. All my attempts to be more or better ground to a halt. All I wanted was to give up. I didn't want to battle, fight and thrash any more. I wanted it all to stop—the constant internal commentary, fantasy criticisms, self-righteous opinions, judgements, and threat of death I held over my head. I just wanted me back, without all of that, without the rules and resolutions, without the shadows of trauma, self-hatred or past mistakes. I wanted to be this, whatever I was in each moment. Paradoxically, giving up the notion of healing was healing in itself.

I was caught in the tidal ebb and flow between the wounding, the no, and my desire to say yes to life. Oscillating between them, I opened and closed, resisted and allowed. I fought against being myself while longing for it. I said no while yearning to say yes. This conflict undid me. I wished for the courage to leap blindly into the oncoming path of life. Gradually I grew more courageous. Being in the dark night, facing ourselves to this depth, is one of the bravest things we will ever do, yet I didn't feel brave. I often found it challenging to do even the most basic tasks and felt weak, inadequate, scared and isolated. But bravery is not defined by the absence of fear. My courage built little by little, and after four years or so I found myself participating in life a little more despite my fears. Even the fighting had not been in vain. It strengthened my will and resolve, building the muscle to be more present to myself.

As the adapted self unravels, it is easy to buy into the idea that certain aspects of mind or thinking are a problem, especially when painful thoughts plague us. At times, my mind was like a Gothic horror show, full of catastrophe, phantasms and bogeymen. Try as I might to silence or modify my thinking, such attempts were rarely successful, not least because thought arises spontaneously and cannot often be controlled by will or effort. Yet painful thoughts, overwhelming though they may become at times, are only a fraction of what the mind conveys. The mind acts as a conduit for everything contained within, including our soul selves. Through it, we hear the wisdom of the mythical and archetypal realms.

The mask depends on our estrangement from the body, its no and all the unruly feelings and sensations of the real self. It can feel as if to engage with, let alone begin to feel all of that, will spell disaster. Paradoxically, it is only when we begin to feel it all that our minds and bodies begin to integrate a little more. The mind is freed of the burden of endlessly having to find solutions to problems it alone perceives. Adrift and anchorless since it staged its inadvertent coup and put itself in charge, the mind discovers that the connection it has been howling for is within the body. The body, no longer continuously at the behest of the mind, makes its needs and desires known. It wants us to know how precious it is.

As the inner dialogues continued, a rapprochement began to emerge. As I listened to each voice, the storm began to quiet. The war within gradually became less intense and in occasional moments, forgiveness and understanding arose effortlessly. Inner coherence developed when I stayed with each part in turn, in the way it demanded in each moment. Slowly, the inner critic softened. The voices within grew kinder, less shrill and more harmonious. My relationship to them changed. I no longer believed everything I heard in my head or instantly reacted to the tales of woe, the warnings, forebodings and exhortations. I had believed that I needed to do what I was told, that it was a serious matter, of life and death. I saw how flimsy it was, fragments picked up hither and thither, pieces learnt from parents, siblings, teachers and friends. All of it second-hand, borrowed, as it was for them, too. I came to honour and appreciate all aspects of my psyche, including my thinking. I realised how hard my mind had tried to help me, as Sutra Ray describes:

> The mind is just so willing. "I'll fix it. Let me help." I feel like really bowing to that. I really understood the effort of my conditioning trying to serve me.[24]

---

[24] Sutra Ray, in conversation.

I began to recognise my innate needs and rhythms for the first time. I had believed I had to keep up with others and the world. I had tried hard to keep up with my inner taskmaster. Now I could no longer bury my head in the sand and deny what was true for me. I stopped keeping up—catastrophically. I was often at odds with my superego, some of the people around me and society at large. Letting go of the precepts and beliefs I had lived by was no easy task. It was my body that often led the way. Activities that were not right gave rise to a strong somatic response. I tried to go back to my old profession and felt physically dreadful the moment I stepped back in that direction. I needed to stick to my own rhythm, and still do. I needed to take time out, stop the doing or keeping up, sit in silence or darkness, move in spontaneous and uncodified ways. I had to learn anew how to be in each moment.

The lost, fragmented parts of my psyche began to feel safe enough to make themselves known. Much like a hedgehog, they prickled with defensiveness, still pained by my abandonment of them, and required gentle coaxing and kindness as they emerged. My five or six-year-old self, mistrusting and not sure I would keep my word, wanted to know why it had taken me so long to return to her:

> *I couldn't get you to listen. I thought it had all gone wrong. I've been so frightened. I thought you'd left me here and were never coming back and I'd die. I hate you for what you've done to me. I want to come out now. I just wasn't ready before. I'm sorry, I just wasn't ready. Hence all the distracting and avoiding and holding back and evading and dipping-one-toe-in-the-watering. I didn't want to be seen. I was in hiding, playing safe.*

In the twenty years prior to the dark night, I had come to understand my patterning or conditioning to some extent. I had even been through a precursor experience, a period in my late twenties and early thirties[25] when the lid had come off—as I described it then—and my suppressed childhood pain had begun to emerge. It was at this time that I began the spiritual quest, trying to find the ultimate healing, something that would fix me for good. But the therapeutic processes I had engaged in, however deep they felt at the time, had been filtered through and limited by the nature of my adapted self. Certainly, all my previous work paled by comparison to what happened during the dark night. I was taken apart piece by piece. It was a ruthless process that left no stone unturned. I tried to hold on to bits of myself. *Not this, not that.* But there was no bargaining with the dark night. The persona, used to having its way, struggled with its inability to manipulate the experience. That was precisely the point. I was taken to a place of surrender. True surrender, by its very nature, cannot be conditional.

My beliefs came to light, one after another, in a process that is still underway. I saw that my persona would hold onto even the most painful beliefs because holding onto the known felt safer than facing the unknown. One day, I realised I had always believed that, whatever the circumstances, things were my fault. That's why I had been so defended, argumentative, wound up, held. That's why I had been trying to make it all better. That was the huge secret I had been carrying and defending. No wonder I felt I

---

[25] This experience is often referred to as Saturn's return.

was being criticised. No wonder I continually had fantasy conversations in my head defending myself against the criticisms I thought were being levelled at me. It was because underneath, I felt it was my fault. That was why I hadn't been able to rest or relax—because if I did, the truth would come out.

Underlying all I had done, at the core of my relationship to myself and the world, lay this belief that it was my fault. Now I understood why I had put myself in such hard places, outcast, frightened, without nourishment or support. I also saw that my adapted self was strangely attracted to this belief because it gave me control, a backhanded form of power when I felt powerless. If it was my fault, I somehow became more important, albeit in a negative way. It had been far too painful for me to be consciously aware of these underlying dynamics. It had been less painful to believe everything was my fault, that I was damaged or broken, than it was to feel the raw hurt of what had happened in my childhood.

I saw that the persona operates in a world of polarity. It cleaves to mutually exclusive either/or pairs. "I'm this, not that. I'm not that, I'm this." Living in this either/or world requires tremendous effort. It is exhausting and painful to live in dividedness, always being one and not the other. To maintain this either/or landscape, the adapted self is under constant pressure to do, change, alter, adjust or revise itself, others or the world. It must constantly meddle with experience to make it conform to its own version of reality. The persona must stay loyal to its narrative, even when faced with contrary evidence. No wonder each experience of the real self, however brief, is such a huge relief, giving much-needed respite from the conflict of this-not-that.

I was prised out of this polarised mindset, stripped of practices, beliefs and assumptions. As the persona unravelled, I faced each of my identifications and polarities. In the end, I was left naked. This process took a long time. We are so thoroughly immersed in polarity and embody it so deeply, it is painful to unravel. As Stefano suggests, the key is letting things be, which is easier said than done:

> Hot and cold, right and wrong, this means that—the assignment of labels and judgements. All of it is a constant replaying of old, unfinished business that wants to be healed. When you don't touch it, when you just don't touch it, when you stop and let the nervous system do what it's going to do, you notice that they're judgements, assignments and labels coming from this old, unfinished history. They're nothing to do with now.[26]

As the unconscious material that had underpinned it broke into consciousness, my persona ceased to function, leaving me in limbo. My masks fell away. In fact, at the start of the dark night, my mask literally came off—I spontaneously stopped wearing makeup. Since early adulthood, I had worn eyeshadow and mascara every day. It felt strange yet wholly fitting to be without it, and I didn't wear it again for two years. My desire to be visible in the outside world reduced to virtually zero. Any notions of ambition or achievement disappeared almost completely.

---

[26] Stefano, in conversation.

None of this is to say the self structure as a whole is entirely dysfunctional. Some parts come through unscathed. We are a mosaic of the neurotic and healthy, the normal and the problematic. The persona is the vehicle through which we navigate life, a necessary interface. It is yet another of life's amazing creations, whatever its complexion. In the dark night, I saw the deep innocence in every aspect of it. Any spiritual or religious teaching that denies, condemns or seeks to suppress any facet of our being, including the persona, is patently missing the point.

As I saw, heard and honoured each part, I began to savour the sweetness of my persona, of the movement of self. Attempting to get rid of it or transcend it seems akin to trying to crush a butterfly or cut down a newly sprouted tree. I also started to touch the delicacy and tenderness of the real self more frequently. It is more refined and subtle than the persona. It has a beautiful exquisiteness one must taste to understand. It effortlessly allows the full spectrum of experience. It knows that experiences are, in some mysterious way, equal and equally valid. We all have a memory of this self, sometimes a visual memory, certainly a cellular memory. We were that as very young children, before we had to become a fixed someone, before we had to adapt and became self-conscious. We intimately know the gossamer-fine transparency and the sheer vibrancy and aliveness of the real self, even if we have forgotten it for many decades.

What becomes of the adapted self as it unravels? Rather than being uprooted or destroyed, it undergoes a metamorphosis. Its coarseness and density are transmuted into something altogether more fluid and unbound.

It comes to know itself as part of the whole rather than, as it presumed, an isolated, separate entity adrift from life. It is freed to be itself, however and whatever being itself entails. During the dark night, it goes through a maturation process. As the unfelt pain of the past is met and digested, the persona can release some of its defensiveness, protectionism and perfectionism. True maturity, we discover, comes when we include, rather than exclude, every part of ourselves, allowing each part to integrate naturally. The mature ego recognises its needs and holds its boundaries. It takes itself less seriously than before yet knows its own truth and power. It is tempered by a natural compassion for itself and others. And it can still don an appropriate mask whenever it needs to, knowing it is not the mask. Consciously putting on a front when required is very different from believing we *are* that front.

As this evolution continued, my individual personality quirks and talents shone more clearly. The adapted self had hidden my brightness. The energy held in rigidity and posturing slowly freed up, and I became more creative, truer to myself. I began to do and be more naturally. Life became simpler when I no longer tried to push the river. Over and over again, I found myself truly undone. And still it goes on, this never-ending cycle of disentanglement and reconnection.

This unravelling of the persona is a profound and at times deeply unsettling process. It can be helpful to have some intellectual understanding of the personality structure and the forces that go into its making. There are many maps and theories that may resonate with you.

Personally, some knowledge of attachment theory, neurosis, transpersonal psychology and the Enneagram of Personality helped me to understand and navigate with a little more ease. By reading about such things, it became clear that what I was experiencing was, while unique to me, also emblematic of the human condition. Somatic inquiry and deep psychotherapy were supportive at various times, as were interventions that gently held my system as it unwound. Again, this is a matter of individual experimentation. You may find books or other resources on any aspect of psychology, spirituality or related fields that give you succour.

During the dark night, it is wise to be as discerning as you can about the company you keep in both the physical and virtual worlds. Desperate as you will feel at times to be rescued, fixed, delivered or numbed, beware those offering simplistic, certain fixes. When the self seems to be the cause of all your suffering, teachings that categorically state there is no self may be beguiling. When what happened feels unbearable, the idea that nothing happened feels like balm. Many are the temptations of the spiritual marketplace, selling no end of solutions to suffering and glittering states to reach. Whenever you feel you have arrived at an answer, the paradoxical nature of life will show you what you have missed or overlooked. Eventually, you become your own authority. As the adapted self unravels, you realise you are not only this limited, concrete, definable self you thought you were. Your glorious, never-to-be-repeated, magnificent, whole self becomes ever more apparent.

Mature spirituality does not seek to deny, remove or transcend any aspect of ourselves. It certainly never shames, lectures, harangues, criticises or blames. It takes us into the reality of ourselves, enabling us to deepen more fully into whatever is here. It facilitates a deeper communion with all aspects of life and speaks to our souls. Keep looking and you will find what you need.

Chapter Five: Transmuting Our Pain

In the house of distraught:
I saw the word "distraught" today
and my body said "Yes,
I thought you'd never notice."

In the dark night, I felt the pain of the events that had shaped my persona, the pain I had presumed was wrong, unacceptable and without value, the pain I had tried to expunge. I felt pain that others had inflicted on me: betrayals, criticism, harm. I felt pain I had inflicted on myself: self-betrayals, self-criticism, self-harm. I recognised the pain I had inflicted on others. Deep down, even though I had believed I had to repress or deny my real self, I had also longed to reconnect with it. I was terrified it was lost or gone forever. By feeling the pain, I eventually found myself. I also discovered the untold preciousness within the pain itself. A part of me had kept my pain precious and safe, even as I had despised it, ignored it, punished it, avoided it and distracted myself from it. I had been ashamed of my most precious parts—softness, vulnerability and gentleness. I was grateful to my soul for holding them for safekeeping until I could make this descent to retrieve them.

Intuitively, I had always known there was something precious within the pain. I instinctively knew my lost self was inextricably bound to it. I had found a sort of refuge in my pain, carefully curating it, sanctifying and unconsciously identifying with it. It was almost as if I became the pain in an effort to retrieve what I had lost. I hid in the pain and earnestly nurtured it. Everything I did subtly engendered or perpetuated the pain. I invested in it, loved it and was enthralled by it. I got so trapped in it that it became my only option. Unsurprisingly, I didn't want to give it up. I had held onto it for so long because I thought I had to in order to survive. I resisted its loss. I certainly didn't want to lose the anger. I was angry at the prospect of losing the anger. I did not know myself without the pain, so the idea of losing it struck a chord of fear:

> *There's no way I'm letting go of it all. I wouldn't be me. I've put so much care and attention to detail into it. Retelling, many times over. Remembering. I want to keep it all. It's spellbinding, enamouring. I want to keep what others don't want. Suffering gives me purpose and fulfilment. Do not take my pain away from me. I have built a monument to it.*

The experiencing of emotion in the dark night has a breathtaking depth and physicality to it. We connect with the realness of long-held pain as if feeling it for the first time, even though we may have made contact with it many times before. We descend into it, inhabiting it in a way far removed from our previous encounters with it. We are very much in the raw experience of the present, yet what is present is the past, or a fragment of it. Here, time has stood still. Petrified, frozen parts of ourselves have awaited our return. Their aliveness, vehemence and truth are stunning. We become them. They speak through us, reanimated. Sometimes when I wrote, my handwriting morphed into that of my child self as she expressed her pain.

Whatever our particular histories and wounds, we are unceremoniously taken back to all our unavowed hurts and traumas. Memories and other images appear, as do long-silent voices and visceral emotions and sensations. Gone is the terrain of cognition or intellect. This is the ancient landscape of weeping and wailing, feral raging and primal fear. We can only let it come, just as it does.

When I was seventeen, my friend Alice died in an accident, a loss I thought I had mourned. One day some thirty years later, I found myself there again. It felt like grief would tear me apart. I wept and wanted to pull my hair and keen and rock like women from less repressed cultures do. I had been so sad—and scared to stop and face it. I didn't think I could have fun, love or happiness after her death. I'd been bracing myself, waiting for it to happen again. As I wept, I realised it was not going to happen again. It happened in 1979, and it was tragic and very shocking, especially to a group of seventeen-year-olds. And nobody talked about it afterwards. I wanted to scream and scream and scream: "No! This girl existed! She lived for eighteen years and she was beautiful and clever and soft and easily startled and funny, and she was my best friend and I loved her." It had freaked me out that nobody would talk about her, as if denying her existence. I had stopped trusting life. As I sobbed for her, swathes of some other, unnameable grief came, maybe from a time before my incarnation, maybe from my parents or grandparents or further-back ancestors.

There is nothing indulgent about being with our pain in this way. It is not a wallowing or a holding on. Rather, it is a declaration, an admission of what is already present. When we finally *feel* what is here in its absolute fullness—rather than talking about it, observing it, or trying to make it better—it transmutes into something rich and ultimately beautiful. We also begin to realise just how much of it there is. The immensity of our wounding cannot be understated. Yet this is also where our deep humanity resides. As we connect with our pain with complete authenticity, compassion inevitably arises. How can it not?

This was the pain I had spent a lifetime trying not to feel, yet ultimately not feeling the pain was more painful than feeling it. There had been times when denial was my only option, when for the sake of my psychological survival it had been better to save it for some later, safer time. But the price of continually trying not to feel was high. Numbing myself to the pain had deadened me. My personal denial was but another drop in the collective ocean of denial in which we find ourselves, the endemic madness of denying our pain and thus heaping ever more agony on ourselves and each other. Even though we fear that the pain will make us crazy, not feeling it has already fractured our psyches. Trying not to feel had made me mad, not an all-out, screamingly bonkers kind of mad, but a socially acceptable, contained kind of mad, a busy-at-work-so-I-don't-feel-the-pain madness. Nearly everything I did was about not feeling the pain. Feeling the pain brought tenderness. I touched the beauty in my vulnerability, my deep insecurity, my utter frailty. I stumbled uncertainly. A whisper came from inside: "You can put it down now. I know you doubt, and I know trust is hard to come by, but really, you can put it all down, right here."

Any notions or beliefs I had about what to feel or how to be, any spiritual, political or psychological ideas I had about what was correct or not, were gradually obliterated. The dam had burst and the waters took their own course. Anger, hatred, grief, envy, rage, shame, guilt, whatever I had repressed in the name of politics, spirituality, self-preservation or self-righteousness, came out. This was an affront, or at least a challenge, to my adapted self. But to my deeper self and my body, experiencing it all authentically at last was often radically energising. Fury took hold:

> *I'm sick of having patience. How could you do that to me? Make me feel safe and then … wham! I trusted you, you fucker. Inside—raging, wild—I died a little every day to save you from the offence of having to take me as I am.*

During the dark night, what has never been spoken is given voice. What has never been told is finally heard. Our truth, such as it is in each moment, emerges. This uncensored, unvarnished truth often runs counter to the narratives to which we have previously subscribed. It may or may not be palatable to those around us, should we choose to share it. We may doubt ourselves. We wonder if we are being over-dramatic, if it really was like that. It is natural that we debate and question, second-guessing our raw experience. In time, we come to trust it more, to know the scent of truth.

Even those of us who consider ourselves emotionally literate struggle to hold or contain the waves of pain that break as the dark night continues. It was not so much that I was feeling the pain as that it had me, doing whatever it did and letting me go when it was done. Whatever the amplitude of each wave, all I could do was stand at the shore and let it break. It took time to develop my capacity to be with such sheer intensity. I could no longer pacify or negotiate with my pain. It demanded to be known on its own terms, to be acknowledged exactly as it was. In short, it refused to be civilised. At first, I tried more desperately than ever to keep it all in, not really knowing exactly what it was. I had dreams of rushing around trying to close all the gaps, shut all the doors, check all the windows, like Cnut[27] trying to stop the tide. Whatever this was, it shouldn't be let out. One afternoon I had a sense of it rising up out of me into the air. Finally, I could let it go. I began to cry as I saw the world was big enough to take it, that it wouldn't harm the world.

Many different feeling states passed through during the dark night. Gradually I began to discern what I was feeling in any given moment. Naming my feelings helped me feel them more completely. This naming happened naturally. It was not that I was intellectualising or trying to work out what I was feeling, but that I would spontaneously recognise the nature of the feeling. Many times I would sit, uncertain of what I was feeling, and then a word would come and reveal the truth of the feeling. I would look up the words in my old dictionary to marinate in the felt sense of them. As I sat one day, a sentence came to me: "Something here needs to be laid to rest." As I looked to see what needed to be laid to rest, the word "guilt" came and fitted perfectly. In that moment, I knew guilt had always been

---

[27] The eleventh-century king of Denmark who supposedly tried to hold back the tide.

present, but I had not recognised it as such. It had been a dimly felt sensation, barely conscious. Naming it allowed me to acknowledge it, to feel it throughout my system, to feel the bodily sensations of it.

One of the feelings central to the structure of my adapted self was, and is, shame. I had repressed the parts of me that others had shamed— inadvertently or otherwise—and felt ashamed of the continued existence of what I had repressed. The shame of being me was a frequent visitor during my dark night. Being unable to control my emotions or function well in the outside world evoked the shame that had originally given rise to the adapted self. It felt shameful to have all these feelings. The shame was difficult to feel, not least because it felt endemic to my whole being. Every cell of my body, every memory, felt shaped by humiliation. It had misshapen my whole being. Every move, every decision, every action had been an attempt not to feel this mortification. Trying to defend against it had put me in positions where I had been humiliated even further. Every step I took seemed to make it worse, but I couldn't stop taking steps. Touching into the depths of it for the first time, I had no idea how to return from it.

The shame I felt was not only from the long-distant past. The relationship I had entered into a few months before the crash was not going well. It seemed no area of my life, either past or present, was untainted by shame. At times, I felt crippled by it. Its breadth and depth were astounding. It seemed my whole life's architecture was founded upon it:

Drowning in shame all day, in the ducking stool.[28] I made such a bad mistake. I've made so many bad mistakes. Trying not to face the wreckage. I've tried so hard not to feel this feeling all my life. All the diversion and evasion and avoidance and pretence. I hoped. I hoped I'd get better and stop feeling it. This is what I've been holding at bay, and it's taken such hard work. I suspended myself. All those parts of myself subordinated, hidden, abandoned, all so that I could avoid this. I couldn't have this happen again—at almost any cost.

The persona forms in part because when we were very young, there was something we never wanted to experience again, be it shame, grief, fear, rejection, or some other shade of feeling. We seem to become what we believe will protect us from ever having to feel that something again. As we touch the feeling our life has been structured to avoid, it can seem as if we will never get over it, it will never end, and we are nothing but this feeling. It can feel as if everyone and everything around us reflects this feeling back to us in some way. We cannot conceive of being without it, as if it is woven into the fabric of our experience for all time. Ultimately, this is not the case. As we admit its full extent, it begins to move, imperceptibly at first and then more noticeably. Trying never to feel it again has done nothing but keep us in thrall to it.

A deep existential anguish or angst was a central feature of my dark night experience. I found myself awake in the small hours, rigid with unspeakable terror, or awash with anxiety during the daytime for no

---

[28] Ducking or cucking stools were used in medieval times to socially humiliate women and men who were deemed to have transgressed, particularly those suspected of witchcraft.

apparent reason. The intensity of the anguish left little room for reason. It was generally impossible to ascribe it to any particular cause, however hard I tried to make sense of it. Eventually, I came to see it arose from a combination of factors, including past trauma and the persona's horror at its own unwinding. It often seemed to be the harbinger of another wave of previously unconscious emotion. After each wave crashed over me, the anguish would subside for a while, giving me a few hours or days reprieve. When it was at its peak, I was at a complete loss. There was nothing I could do. I felt frozen, completely stuck. I had no idea how to move, relax, or flow. It was a really hard place to be:

> *My intense distress as I lay here last night. And now sitting here this morning. Such intense anguish. All of it here, and I really don't want it to be. I really, really want to feel okay. What is it that I need? What would solve this? How do I get away from this? The fear, anguish, intensity, shame. Not this, not this. This is too much. Maybe it'll improve over the course of the day. Maybe it'll open up. Maybe there will be space for it, for me. This horrible, horrible feeling. I wouldn't wish it on my worst enemy. Let's hope it begins to fade. Let's hope it improves. I really need it to get better. Please. Please. Please.*

Desperation was anguish's close companion. I was desperate to get out of the pain. I desperately tried to keep it all together even as it was falling apart. In truth, I had been desperate well before the dark night began. Previously quiet and muted, the desperation was now screaming, unable to be silenced any longer. It felt as if my persona were built on a bedrock of desperation. I reeked of it. The ever-present sense of it permeated everything. Desperation was the gravity around which I revolved. I had tried to shape a me around the desperation, as if the me weren't the desperation itself. It was so old, conditioned, encrusted and habituated. I had turned away from desperate people because desperation was the last thing I wanted to feel. Now here I was.

Desperation in turn gave rise to hopelessness. It all felt hopeless— I felt like a hopeless case. It felt hopeless to try to do anything. Even feeling the hopelessness felt hopeless. At times, I became mired in hopelessness, in my very own slough of despond.[29] There were moments when feeling hopeless felt preferable to feeling anything else, when collapsing into the quicksand of dejection was all I could do. Better to be in the stagnant swamp of hopelessness than to feel anguish, fear or shame. In this place, I met pointlessness and futility. Nihilism reared its head, asserting the meaninglessness of life, the emptiness of all belief, the lack of anything good:

> *No wonder I am drawn to withdrawing from the whole lot. The utter fucking pointlessness of all endeavour, the utter futility of life. No wonder we are driving ourselves to the edge of extinction. Bring it on. Don't pretend you don't know the utter futility of this, deep down. "What is the fucking point?" I ask God, mockingly. I learnt how to function—kind of—despite the crushing futility. I feel the supreme pointlessness of me. No wonder I had to create an elaborate fiction of specialness.*

---

[29] The Slough of Despond is a bog in John Bunyon's book *Pilgrim's Progress*, written in 1678.

The dark night finds ways to bring us into unavoidable contact with unmet trauma. Sophie found herself with no choice but to live with her mother again after decades of independence, a move that took her right back into the trauma of her childhood.

> I went home and lived with my mother, which was brilliant because it was facing all of that childhood trauma again, but as a forty-year-old adult. I was struggling so fucking badly, but I needed to be with it to see where that early patterning, the whole ancestral patterning, came from. It was like having the opportunity to be more of a grownup with it, to come to a place to have compassion towards my mother for her brutality towards me when I was going through this huge spiritual transformation and floundering and practically dying. I was so tired for about three years after that and during that as well. I guess that was me struggling against the process but also having been so tired of driving myself. I still had my mother's voice inside me because it was the earliest voice I heard, so it would echo around me. I had that layered on top of the trauma I was going through. It's really heartbreaking, the lack of trust.[30]

Many of us have experienced trauma, even if we have not recognised it as such. When it irrupts into consciousness, it can feel terrifying and disorientating. We may have had to shut down at some time in the past because the trauma was too much to bear. Under those conditions, we survived by fighting, fleeing, freezing or dissociating. Candace describes her experience:

---

[30] Sophie, in conversation.

It's interesting the amount of effort it takes to shut down our aliveness. I had a really traumatic childhood, so the awakening for me has been messy. I remember being about six or seven, and I would have this dream of a box. The box was getting smaller and smaller and smaller, and it was closing in on me. I would be screaming. That was a recurring dream that I had throughout my life. I was being closed in on. That dream has been so symbolic. That was actually what was happening within my own psyche. I was closing in on myself and containing all of that. Even at such a young age, that came out in a dream. An image of a box.[31]

All of it got boxed up. All the emotions, bodily reactions and sensations we couldn't feel at the time were saved for later. As the box opens, we encounter a range of intense feelings and sensations, as well as memories and thoughts. It is our very own Pandora's box.[32] Whatever its contents, the box, once opened, cannot be permanently sealed again. Sobbing, shaking, wailing, whimpering, trembling—our bodies feel it all. Having spent our lives thus far ensuring the box stays locked, we doubt our ability to survive its opening.

As I have said, we have an innate sense that the contents of the box are precious as well as painful. Indeed, we are terrified we have lost what is precious, that we may not be able to retrieve the most valuable parts of ourselves. We had to lock the box so tightly we doubt our ability to reopen it. Even in the most traumatic circumstances, our soul or psyche

---

[31] Candace, in conversation.

[32] In Greek mythology, Pandora was given a jar containing all the evils of the world. When she opened the lid, the evils spilt out.

keeps it all hidden until we are able to make this descent. It makes sense that as the box opens we experience all the pain and trauma that gave rise to its creation. Along with the pain, precious contents emerge: vulnerability, gentleness, verve, creativity, curiosity, aliveness, wonder and sensitivity. We cannot close selectively, so we close to all of it. This closing in renders us confined and deadened.

I experienced the box as an entity or object within, usually located in my chest or belly. It was heavily guarded at all times, its contents howling ever more loudly as I inched closer to it. It remained determined not to let me near; its existence depended on keeping me locked out. It didn't want me to see beneath it. Its job was to block everything out. It created a kind of painful numbness, cloaking everything. It put me in stalemate. "You are not coming in," it said.

I intensely resisted its opening. I held out as long as humanly possible. Any notion I had about needing to let go merely added more resistance. I went through alternating cycles of resisting and allowing, defending and surrendering. Finally, I saw that all the resistance and repression had been an attempt to look after myself. I had tried to stop life from hurting and tried to deal with it, but it wasn't playing ball. It just hurt. As I let it hurt, the sense came that I could stand down. I didn't have to be vigilant any longer. There was a loosening of the grip, a lessening of the intensity, an allowing of what was here. No wonder I hadn't known how to stop. How would a fighter know anything other than fighting?

There was no way I could or should prematurely prise open the box or yank out its contents. This was slow, painstaking retrieval work. Millimetre by millimetre, the box gradually revealed its precious contents, and in the process, I realised I was being enlivened rather than destroyed. Gradually, despite my doubts and fears, I came to know that the feelings were survivable, even if they felt overwhelming.

Our cultures and family systems teach and sometimes encourage us to minimise certain aspects of our experience. Depending on gender, race, ethnicity, class, creed, sexuality or disability, different or double standards apply. Stereotypes and prejudices circumscribe us, distorting our individuality. In the dark night, whatever we have minimised or denied becomes apparent. Whatever others have belittled or we have downplayed in order to fit in, or at least to avoid conflict or harm, surfaces remorselessly. I've known men who played the tough guy all their lives suddenly awash with vulnerability and fear, incapable of action. I've known women with calm, steady personas who have encountered murderous, spitting-and-cursing rage. We have inevitably contorted ourselves to adapt, pulling ourselves out of our natural shapes in order to survive in the world. Eventually, our souls rebel against the contortions, wrenching us back into our rightful shapes, come what may.

Denial comes in many forms, some masquerading as spiritual practices. Trying to think positively or affirm our way out of what we feel is a classic form of denial. Homilies about others being worse off as a way to diminish or deny our own pain; incessant gratitude practices; using activities or methods as a way to stave off what we are feeling—we find many ways to deny what is here. Regardless of what we tell ourselves, our bodies do not lie. In the dark night, any attempts to bypass what is present are at best fruitless and at worst downright infractions against ourselves. As we feel what is here in all its rawness, we begin to acknowledge every aspect of our experience, free from the taint of judgement or comparison.

I grew up in a tense atmosphere of argument and mistrust. I was twelve when my parents divorced, and I didn't see my father again for six or seven years. As a teenager, I told myself their split had made me independent and self-sufficient, until evidence to the contrary made it clear that was not the whole story. In the dark night, I connected even more deeply with the young Fiona who had not been able to tell anyone, not even herself, how it really was for her.

> *After he went, I wanted to shout, scream, fall apart, and tell people: "My daddy's gone. My daddy's gone, and I don't know where he is." I missed him so much. I didn't understand, truly. I feel the slow, dawning horror. The griefless grief, the absent mourning. The loss it was impossible to share. He was my daddy and then he was gone, and I was expected to forsake him, to deny him. I had to contort myself so as not to feel the pain of his departure.*

Here, the truth has many facets. Previously denied or unacknowledged aspects of the truth emerge during the dark night. This is not the linear truth of historical narrative. Rather, it is the truth of inner experience, the cell-level knowing of how it was for us. Often, this truth conflicts with what we have been told or what we have believed. When it comes, however, its veracity is undeniable. And it is a deep relief to feel and express it. As we do so, a new truth emerges. Layer upon layer of relative truths are uncovered. A rigorous and ongoing honesty is demanded of us. What exactly is here and real in this moment? Yesterday's veracity may not hold true today. When the persona can no longer deny or refute reality, the body is free to feel it all, and the pain runs bone-deep. Initially, I couldn't bear to look within. I didn't want to see the devastation I assumed was there. After a while, I felt the desire to tell the truth; no more playing it down, making light of it, or evading. The raw, eviscerating truth was that I was both utterly devastated and startlingly whole.

The pain we are in the process of transmuting is not entirely personal. Some of it comes from generations past, from all that has been unfelt in our families, tribes and communities. We bear the scars and traumas of our ancestors. This process is deeply challenging in societies in which there is so much denial of pain, and in which emotional pain is deemed to be a purely individual affair and pathologised as madness or illness. We may even touch what feels like the pain of past lives. Whatever our beliefs about such matters, we may see images and feel feelings from places and times removed from our personal experience.

Whatever the exact nature of our histories, we have experienced heartbreak. And we partake of humanity's heartbreak as well as our own broken-heartedness. How can we not be heartbroken by what we witness around us? How can we remain undevastated by the cruelty, grief, degradation and violence we see in the world? To be truly human is to be utterly heartbroken in the face of it all. We create beliefs, stances, strategies and defences in order not to feel the overwhelming, bittersweet sorrow of human suffering. I understand why we try to cut ourselves off from it, but there is really no chance of succeeding, because we are it. When we realise that, our desperate attempts to prove that we are somehow immortal end. There's no way out. Nothing is left out, however ghastly, mundane, or sublime. We touch the profound, inexplicable beauty and deep love for life and humanity that course through us. Life claims us as one of its own.

There comes a time when we are all in. The pain we imagined would destroy us becomes our greatest resource. It is transmuted from what we presumed to be a base, unworthy substance into something immeasurably precious. One of the side effects of this process is a natural compassion for both ourselves and others. When we intimately know our own pain, when we have stepped over the hot coals of our own suffering time and time again, we come to know the terrain well enough to walk alongside our fellow travellers.

As the adapted self unravels, we feel the pain that is its very fabric, the pain it has protected us from. As we feel the pain, the adapted self is digested or integrated, no longer propped up by unfelt or unconscious pain. It is a seismic shift from trying not to feel the pain to allowing it to be there. It goes against the persona's grain, but in the dark night it has no choice. It knows that feeling this pain will be its ultimate undoing, and yet we also long to discover what is most deeply real within us. We know in our hearts that who and what we purport to be is not our real selves.

The waves of pain can be ferocious and intense. We may do everything in our power to numb, solve, deflect or avoid them. It can feel as if our bodies have taken on lives of their own, as if they are rebelling against us. We have minimal ability to impose order on or calm our inner experience during the dark night. Obviously, this is frightening and disturbing. We are called to do what was previously unthinkable and simply let it all happen. The deep intelligence of the soul is at work and it cannot be second-guessed or managed. The waves will come just as they do, regardless of our wishes or designs. As Stefano says:

> You're at the train station, you sit on that bench, and guess what? Those trains are going to come through, and you ain't going to do a damn thing about it. That train wants to come through because the nervous system is wired to heal itself. It has an inherent self-correcting mechanism and that train needs to come through. Hold the space, let it run and don't touch it. It's okay, you can feel it, it's not going to kill anybody, you're still going to be here afterwards. Just feel that shit, don't worry about it. Drop into your body.[33]

This is a fine art. It takes practice to get the balance right, neither meddling with the pain nor holding it at bay. There will be times when you try to hold back the train with every ounce of effort you can summon. That is all part of the process. Most of the time, the waves simply crash or ripple ashore, and you find yourself submitting to them in whatever fashion happens in the moment. The invitation is, to use Stefano's phrase, "not to

---

[33] Stefano, in conversation.

deny or indulge." Gradually, as we experience for ourselves that the feelings are survivable, we calm a little and dramatise less. We begin to experience our experience, whether painful or pleasurable, in a less conditional way. We need to eke out time and space to be with ourselves as best we can. For Per, there was a time when he had no choice but to walk:

> After maybe two or three years I started getting this extremely strong sense of dread and terror. It was with me the whole time. I couldn't sleep. The only thing I could do was walk in the forest, and I did that every day, for the whole day, basically. There were other things coming up—memories, traumas, things that wanted to be processed and seen. Walking was definitely my main support. I walked for hours every day.[34]

I found myself lying on the sofa or the floor for long periods of time. I walked, paced, cried, rocked, and sat still. Music was one of my greatest supports. A song would unexpectedly tap into the state I was in, cradling the emotion as it came forth. I would play the same track over and over until I was spent. A particular song would resonate for a while, then my state would change and it would no longer arouse the same response. I had no way to predict which songs would speak to me; they were an eclectic mix style-wise. I retain a huge fondness for all these songs. Writing also came naturally at this time, as it did for Luann. What was pouring forth demanded to be seen, written, expressed:

---

[34] Per, in conversation.

My sense was that the self was breaking down, the self that I'd created, which was a lot of falsehoods. I vomited it all out onto the page, over a longer period of time than I cared for. I recall a significant amount of time of vomiting out the wounds that had led to the wound-driven behaviour that created that false self. It was very much a cycle of feeling sick inside, and then going over to the couch and crying and writing. Writing or mind-mapping. I did a lot of that to sort out all that was coming out. I wouldn't always want to be with the pain on the couch, even though I knew I would feel better. Insight after insight, understanding would come. "Oh, no wonder I feel like this." It wasn't just vomiting. It was clarity.[35]

After the initial shocks of the crash and the descent, we begin to acclimatise to the dark night process, such as it is for each of us. Terry describes how this happened for him:

It was a matter of settling into it, not being in a hurry to come out, but just being in it. There'd be little moments where I'd get a couple of hours or half a day when it would lift, and I'd think, "I'm pretty normal today," and then it would come back again. The practical thing for me was hanging on to the consciousness that I am not this experience. There was the ongoing sensation in the body that sometimes seemed almost unbearable. I played a game I called Quantum of Solace. My experience is ninety-nine per cent fucking awful. Maybe there's a one per cent thing—oh yeah, there's a bird singing. The misery hasn't gone away, but one per cent of my attention can just notice, oh my god, there are still blackbirds.

---

[35] Luann, in conversation.

> It was just a tiny quantum of solace that sustained me in the dark period.
>
> Another game I started to play was enjoying the pain. There's this horrible feeling that I'm calling my pain. What if it isn't pain? What if it is actually an extreme, almost erotic pleasure to have this sensation in my body? It's ridiculous, but it's a way of turning it around. There was a number of different things that would work for a while, and then I'd be right in it again. Then I'd just have to be in pain for a while, and then I'd find another little quantum of solace.[36]

It is not necessarily a matter of being in the pain all the time. After a while, once the pain knew I would come back to it and that I wasn't trying to suppress it in any way, it sometimes lifted sufficiently to allow me to function when I needed to, albeit in a limited fashion. It was helpful to realise that some parts of me had remained unaffected. I could still cook a meal or walk the dog. If I tried to avoid the pain for any length of time, however, my ability to function seemed to diminish even further.

There were times when I could abide with the pain and times when I absolutely could not. When there was no way I could be with it, I would watch television for a few hours, ignoring it as best I could. The pain was still there, but the distraction sometimes created a little distance until I could bear it again. Other times, the pain was so intense it occupied my attention entirely, whatever else I tried to do. The fewer ideas I had about how I should be with the pain, the better I fared. When I tried to make my

---

[36] Terry, in conversation.

experience conform to some notion of how things should be, I added yet more layers of judgement, shame and failure to it.

At the beginning of the dark night, I bought into the idea that I was supposed to let go or accept. I thought I was supposed to be doing anything but the thing I was actually doing. I thought I wasn't supposed to be terrified, sad or envious, which made me terrified and sad—and envious of all those who seemed not to be terrified, sad or envious. Trying to be what I was not in any given moment gave rise to a frantic energy that searched desperately for solutions. It was a relief when ideas about who, what or how I was supposed to be finally lost their hold.

Once I understood the dark night was the reclamation of my soul self, I recognised it had its own pace and rhythms. It could and would not be hurried. When I was able to bring my consciousness to what I was experiencing, I discovered a deep sense of intimacy with myself. Regardless of what I was feeling, this intimacy itself felt good. Becoming intimate with my pain brought me closer to my real self than I had been since I was very young. One day, I lay on my bed and realised as I felt into myself that I had surrendered. I'd gathered up all the parts of me and was taking care of them all, rather than rejecting the painful ones. For a while, I had a delicious sense of self. However excruciating it was to feel the pain, it was at times like these I ended up feeling immensely grateful for everything the dark night brought with it.

Chapter Six: Being with Ourselves (and Others)

The dark night came calling because I had innocently and inadvertently left myself. Having been left by others, I had joined in the abandonment, shifting my locus from the real to the outer shell of my being. This self-abnegation was devastatingly painful. I had cast myself out a million times over. Turning against myself had seemed to be the only way I could avoid being utterly alone. A sense of absence permeated my whole being. I was more absence than presence. I was all I had been fighting not to be, lonely and disconnected. I had diligently tried to make up for this enormous hole, and now I was in it. I had totally fallen through the net. Luann was also left with an unbearable sense of nothingness within:

> I had left myself over and over. So when he left and the children were gone half the time, and I had left, there was nobody there. There was nothing in there. I wasn't even there. What do you do with that? How do you live? You can't.[37]

When we realise we are being broken open because we left ourselves, the remedy becomes clear. The only option is to return and be with ourselves as best we can. The word "with" is key here. What is required is our presence, our companioning of ourselves in this place. The dark night is an apprenticeship in being with ourselves in the truth of each moment. We learn how to be with the parts of ourselves that have never been presenced

---

[37] Luann, in conversation.

before, by us or anyone else. Being with ourselves is a far cry from grabbing for techniques or teachings to stem the flow. We each find our unique way, inevitably stumbling as we go.

Nearly all of us have been taught to manage, problem-solve, change or deny our present reality. These are useful skills to have at times. Yet when we are willing to be with whatever is here just as it is, our capacity to be present builds, albeit in a haphazard and roundabout way. Being present is not an all-or-nothing proposition; sometimes it is enough just to be a few per cent present. "Whatever is here" includes resisting, kicking and screaming. It cannot be said often enough that there is no prescription for how to be in the dark night. There is a big difference between witnessing or observing and this kind of full-bodied inhabiting that engages every level of our being. It is a subtle allowing of our whole experience without being in any way outside it. There is nothing studied or forced about it. Sutra Ray says:

> The key word there is "inhabit." To be with something is to inhabit it, join it, be it. To be in the current is-ness, rather than describing or remembering.[38]

As the facade of the false self crumbles and we evolve into the bigger, deeper reality of ourselves, we need time and space to complete the incomplete, to make explicit what has been implicit. Our real self is asking for pure, unalloyed attention. More than anything, we need time to be with

---

[38] Sutra Ray, in conversation.

what is here without concepts and judgements about the process itself. Once the superego quiets a little, it becomes more possible to be with ourselves free of censure. For a long time, I balked at the simplicity of this. I wasn't prepared to jump into being here, preferring instead to try to make the unworkable function, to force sense from the nonsensical, to create reality from fantasy. Eventually, the simplicity and necessity of being with myself became breathtakingly clear. Sophie poetically describes this being with:

> It was a being asked to be with, be with, be with, to come back to, to rest, to be resting in the body, to drop through this. To actually drop into an awareness, to a consciousness, a softness, a love, an inward-going, this being the point where everything happens, this being the love, this being the all of it, the sweet heart of living. This feels like being afforded by grace the opportunity to live in the sweet way, the right way, the way of love and happiness. Being with the immediacy rather than the shadows in the outside world. Being with the direct experience as far as that's possible.[39]

As I learnt to be with myself, I started to notice my ever-present capacity to notice, the consciousness that Sophie referred to. However dire my experience, I was aware of it. I was effortlessly aware and present regardless of what I was aware of or present to. This unchanging awareness or presence is fundamental; it is the essence of our being and the wellspring of life. I noticed its immanent intelligence at work. I began to trust it, a

---

[39] Sophie, in conversation.

little cautiously at first, as I was unaccustomed to its movements. Unlike the intelligence of the intellect, which depends on knowledge, this unnameable intelligence is inherent in being. It infuses both mind and body. As the dark night continued, I came to trust it more deeply than anything else. I found myself ready and willing to cede control in the knowledge that it was holding me:

> *Such open arms, holding me as I fall in trust. This wordless place: so beautiful, quiet, full, alive, playful. The mystery of aliveness, such vastness. I see the sweetness of our humanity, too, so heartbreakingly sweet. We're here. This is true communion; being here with all that is.*

As I began to trust, a sense of resolve emerged. This resolve was firm yet gentle, clear yet undogmatic. There was no element of "should" in it. It was a resolve not to leave myself, to let things pass through without absenting myself. Many years previously I had lost my resolve, and it was what I most needed now. Step by step, piece by piece, I made the commitment to stay with myself and to avoid the temptation to cede to collapse or distraction. Every time I stayed with myself through a wave of pain, it was as if I were regaining my original shape, straightening out the dents and twists caused by the many adaptations made to my structure. I would feel my body move back towards its original contours, relieved at being freed from holding the unnatural postures it had taken on.

We have an innate sense of the qualities of love, kindness and care, even if we have rarely experienced them. In a way, this knowing makes our lives all the more painful; we know what we are missing. I had longed for kindness, yet my inner terrain had often been hard or harsh. I had been excluded from the kindness and compassion I had shown other people over the years. As I began to inhabit my experience, I occasionally connected with a profound, effortless kindness. It's not that I was trying to be kind to myself, but that kindness simply emerged as I stayed true to myself moment by moment. I became my own kin rather than being estranged from myself. As the layers of conditioning fell away, I encountered the qualities that had lain dormant within, obscured by my persona. I began to become what I needed, the older woman I had wanted to look after me.

> *I see and hear a kindly mother figure—me—saying, "Slip your things off. Let's tuck you into bed. I'm going to look after you now." I feel arms around me. I've been out on a limb. Something was severed or separated. I lost the ability to comfort myself. I lost the ability to do what's right for me. I put myself in harm's way. Self-love pours in.*

There were many times, however, when it was impossible to be with myself because what I was experiencing was overwhelmingly painful or unbearable. Initially, I took my inability to be present as yet more evidence of my inadequacy. Over time, I came to see the idea that we should be able to traverse this territory entirely on our own as callous and risible. Much as the dark night requires periods of solitude, it is also immeasurably helpful to be in the company of those who can be present with us as we feel the pain, *anam cara* or soul friends who can hold space for us with no agenda of their own.

Being with those who can meet us with kindness and presence creates a sense of trust and safety that we may have rarely experienced. In this safe place, our deepest wounds can begin to be admitted and seen. Spending time with someone who intimately knows this landscape may lessen our fear and loneliness. Connecting with those who can hear, see, understand and validate our experience can be deeply relieving, particularly when we are in the pain of disconnection, of not being seen, heard or understood. Those nearest to us might not have the capacity to do this, understandably enough, so we may need to look further afield for those who can. At the start of my dark night, I sought out two people who I thought might help me understand what I was undergoing. One of them succinctly spelled it out to me in a message I have kept to this day. I came back to his words repeatedly:

> This indeed sounds major. Just try to stay with the process as much as you can and trust that you will be held. Nothing to do except be present to what's happening. A relaxation has taken place on a deep level. The grip is loosened and thus a collapse is occurring. However, the collapse is of the false, of the unreal.[40]

Unsurprisingly, the dark night can have a profound effect on our closest relationships, which may end, change or deepen. I experienced times of bone-crushing loneliness, of wondering if I would ever truly connect with anyone again. I found myself withdrawing from some friendships and

---

[40] Julian, via email.

being drawn to others. Ultimately, we must make this journey alone, because that is its nature. As we journey, we find our connections radically alter. The more deeply we can be with ourselves, the more deeply we can be with others. As we discover the real within ourselves, so we connect with the real in others. Friendships based on the real begin to form and flourish, just as those based on trying to enhance or validate each other's self-image tend to wither on the vine, unless we can reach the depths below. I am sure I was difficult to be with because I was in a different realm, far removed from those around me. I was no longer the person I had been, which was challenging for some of my loved ones. Naturally, it was painful for those who loved me to see me in pain. They had their own responses to what I was experiencing. Some people were kind and supportive, while others were clueless, oblivious or frankly lacking in compassion. For Sophie, dealing with the judgemental reactions of her family was one of the most difficult things about the dark night:

> The dark night deepened my connection with the whole of life, so I'm not satisfied with small talk. I need that kind of depth, but my family cannot relate. I've had "navel-gazing" levelled at me from all over. That's how they talk about it because they can't make sense of it. What they don't see is the fucking heroic journey.[41]

Others' attempts to support us during this time may inadvertently exacerbate our suffering. People around us may be scared by our need for

---

[41] Sophie, in conversation.

solitude and darkness, or alarmed by our expressions of how we feel, so they understandably try to make us feel better. This can compound matters, as Rachel describes:

> People would say, "You'll be alright. You've got all these amazing skills." And I would think, "You don't understand. I can't." As supportive and loving as they were trying to be, it actually made things worse because I felt like I was really failing, and if everybody else could see I could do this, why couldn't I? What was the matter with me? It escalated all that stuff that was already there. I'd never felt so alone and frightened as an adult. It was like being that utterly alone, frightened child again, but thinking I should be able to sort this out because I'm an adult. Just the most humiliating, embarrassing thing...[42]

Gradually, I came to know what and who I needed to be with. I looked for sources of solace and deep wisdom. I wanted a big-hearted elder or mentor who could see me through kind eyes, who could embrace me and teach me true discernment. Still a child, I wanted to meet wisdom, to touch its words on the dark night air, to sit by its feet and drink from its cup. I found myself seeking out soul nourishment wherever I could. It seemed hard to come by, most of the time. But "seek, and ye shall find."[43] Sustenance came from the unlikeliest of sources—chance encounters with strangers, films, music, talks with friends, art, scriptures, poetry, nature. I would stumble unexpectedly across wisdom. It was a question of letting myself look

---

[42] Rachel, in conversation.
[43] The Bible. Luke chapter 11 verse 9.

wherever and however I looked, rather than limiting my scope by having fixed ideas about what I needed and where it could be found.

As I stayed with myself, I began to connect with the wisdom I sought and hear its words directly. I realised it was also inherent within me. Clearly, wisdom is not contained or owned by any one person, tradition or teaching. It flows as it does. Eventually, I began to follow wisdom's promptings most of the time. This did not necessarily look adult or spiritual, but it felt sacred. I began truly to listen to what spoke to me and respond to what drew me. I didn't always like what I heard. At times it was inconvenient or challenging. Gradually, the idea of looking outside myself for what I believed was missing within became moot, yet I continued to partake of the wisdom of others and find rich sources of nourishment and soul connection along the way.

Many of us become reclusive during the dark night. Simply existing may feel like all we can do. Interacting and relating are beyond our capacity at times, especially if no one in our vicinity recognises or understands where we are. Our instinct—like an injured creature—is to withdraw in seclusion and tend to our wounds. Luann speaks about her reclusive period:

> One of the parts was being a recluse, not wanting at all to be part of society because I didn't feel safe out there. I was already in so much pain, I couldn't stand to be re-wounded.[44]

---

[44] Luann, in conversation.

This desire to withdraw from the external world is entirely natural during the dark night. We need to follow the pull downwards and inwards. In our own way, we follow the mystics and poets of all traditions who have withdrawn from society to live simple, contemplative lives—the Desert Fathers and Mothers, sadhus, hermits and Sufis, to name a few. Difficult as it is in current times, we find ways to cloister. For some, ill health leaves no choice but to live a secluded life. Whatever our circumstances, we gradually find ways to balance our external responsibilities with this visceral, undeniable need for silence, stillness and contemplation. However necessary the time and space we carve out for ourselves, it can feel illicit and transgressive. I loved sitting with myself, music on, dark outside, soaking in the intimacy of one. Those were the moments I savoured most. They felt a little like they had been stolen. We may even feel selfish for needing this intimacy with ourselves. Anja describes her need for silence and how it is sometimes at odds with the needs of others in her life:

> What feels the best for me is silence. I don't feel like talking with a lot of people. I just really want to be with me. It starts with just being with me, and then something can come through. It is difficult being in relationships or friendships, or with the [adult] children.[45]

Many of us have been socialised to put others' needs ahead of our own. The dark night breaks down such conditioning. That is not to say we stop

---

[45] Anja, in conversation.

caring, or that we do not continue to fulfil our responsibilities towards others, even though to do so may be deeply challenging at times. As we become truer to ourselves, so we allow others to be themselves in a way that the adapted self simply couldn't countenance. Our relationships are recalibrated in a variety of ways.

This is the time for cocooning. In fact, the struggle within the confines of the dark night cocoon precedes our eventual emergence. While we are in the cocoon, we can neither foretell nor plan our ultimate form, the shape we will one day take. Living in buy-it-now, quick-fix cultures has made us impatient, but this is an alchemical transmutation that cannot be forced or expedited. It will take the time it takes. The fermentation of the soul takes years, not weeks. We gradually become patient and learn how to savour the process of soul ripening. We begin to understand the direction of the journey, whatever its course in each moment. Even though we try to resist the movement at first—it feels counterintuitive to move towards pain rather than away from it—we come to realise that is exactly what is required. Rather than moving out, all we need do is come in to it all—the body, thoughts, feelings. It is a slight, subtle movement.

Our bodies have inevitably borne the brunt of the false self's skewed perspectives. The persona tends to judge the body harshly, comparing it to what and how it believes it should be. It is too this, not enough that. Since my early teenage years, whenever my body was as I desired it to be, I felt pride in it. When it wasn't, I shamed it and myself. Having had disordered eating as a young woman, I had a fractious relationship with my body. I had separated myself from it and attempted to control it, corral it and bend it to my will. Its natural functions humiliated me. In my family, talking about them had been taboo. I had denied my body's reality for so long—its peeing, farting, shitting, bleeding, sliming reality—it was shocking to finally realise what I had done to it. Suddenly, it was present and real. I had been pretending it wasn't and had tried to keep it quiet. In fact, I had wanted to get rid of it. It couldn't do enough to please my perfectionist persona:

> *I've been trying to deny my body. Such harsh, barren, sterile conditions. Sensory deprivation. I've been so cut off from my body. I thought I wasn't my body, that I was somehow above it—superior to it—and that's been so painful. The body is included too. How preposterous, the idea that I'm not this. Now, I just want to be here, in this body, with all that it does. I just want to lie still, very, very still. My body knows what to do, but I didn't trust my body. I thought my body had betrayed me. In fact, I betrayed my body, over and over. I thought I wasn't supposed to have limits or fears.*

Being with our bodies, reuniting with our bodies rather than denying them, seems to run counter to the spiritual teaching that we are not the body. That teaching, in my view, reinforces the pernicious belief that mind and body are separate. Transcendent, patriarchal religions and spiritual teachings have preached the sinfulness of the body—particularly the female body—for millennia. The belief that spirit and matter are separate has permeated our cultures, creating enormous torment. When we feel separate from our bodies, we are separate from our experience. In fact, separation *is* our experience. To inhabit the reality of our bodily experience is radical. We tend to be tied to our various conventions and rulebooks, our fixed ideas of how we are supposed to be with our experience. The dark night takes us beyond all that. We come out of confinement, leaving the rigidity of practice behind. We begin to move less formulaically, less apologetically.

The more embodied we become, the less separate we feel. The greater the unity of mind and body, the more whole and alive we feel. Paradoxically, the more embodied we become, the less identified with our bodies we are. We come to see that mind and body are not two distinct things. As I listened to my body, I appreciated its wisdom more and more. It was clearly saying that I was not this outer shell, this mask or adapted self. I'd not heard it because I had been ignoring it. Finally, I gave it my attention:

> *None of it is me. I've tried so hard to find me in something, and I've tried so hard to find something in me. I've been trying so hard to prove that isn't me, I don't know what is me. I am this (the last thing I wanted to be). What will happen if I am this? I'll come home, and that will be almost unbearably painful, as everything in me was trying not to be this. I just am this. What will happen if I just am this? It'll be so much less effort, and I'll have time to live. I could just live, like I did when I was little, and I was just being me.*

When I could be with the body and its experience, all that had been denied could emerge. When I stopped trying not to feel, the defences against my body and all it contained gave way. No wonder I had looked frantically for help, casting about for solutions. I thought I would die. I thought I needed to do something radical. My pain felt unsolvable, and I desperately wanted a solution. I spent a long time looking for some kind of resolution. From this perspective, it was hard to believe the best thing I could do was nothing. The notion of letting things be seemed utterly nonsensical. However, I gradually came to realise that all my attempts to find a solution to myself had come to naught. The only solution was to be with it all; that was the radical thing I needed to do. Amazingly, I found myself surviving the onslaughts of feeling time and time again. I came to appreciate both mind and body for the utterly miraculous phenomena they are. Tenderness was possible when I let the body do its bodying while the mind minded.

During the dark night, fluctuating tides carried me between presence and absence. These tides continue to exert their force. The movement into the unknown was tempered by a desire to stay in the familiar, hazy world of avoidance and enactment. The dead weight of denial exerted a strong gravitational pull. I tried hard to stay asleep. I wanted to stay on the surface, to be distracted. Despite all my protestations to the contrary, my claims that I wanted to awaken more than anything, I had to admit that I also longed to stay static and unconscious. Believing myself unstable had brought its own stability. Then I discovered there was no stability, no ground where I could set up shop, no land on which to stake my claim.

Being with what is most real takes practice and commitment. Having spent so long removed from my direct experience I needed to relearn exactly how to be present. I explored various ways of being with my somatic and imaginal selves, the wholeness of myself. I derived little benefit from structured practices. Instead I immersed myself in a more organic, free-flowing way of being with the stream of experience as it came. When I stopped trying to work things out intellectually, insights and realisations came spontaneously. I found myself inquiring in a fluid, effortless, organic way. The layers of the false self began to peel away as I dropped ever deeper.

> *After he went downstairs, I lay in bed and was able to just feel it. What came up was the realisation that I need to make it better, that compulsion, always there from when I can remember. And the sense, along with that, that there's something wrong with me. Under that, there's a deep feeling of vulnerability, of wanting to hide.*

As I got used to being with myself in this way, I connected with a profound patience. Despite all my frustration, impatience and struggling, some part of me had been silently and patiently waiting for me to stop all my doing and turn within. Regardless of my avoidance, aversion, diversion and distraction tactics, it was still here. All it needed was time and space. I had been enculturated to be productive, so naturally the idea of taking fallow time ran counter to my conditioning. Yet fallow time was essential. In winter, the soil rests and its fertility is restored. Likewise, during the dark night, we are restored to ourselves, the shedding of the persona creating fertiliser for the growth of our souls.

Being with ourselves in this way is not a passive act. It is not a capitulation or supine surrender; neither does it preclude resistance or protest. Any ideas of needing to take a particular stance towards our experience only serve to compound matters. Being present does not impede the full range of reactions we might have to what is transpiring because we are present to everything. The rigours of the dark night build our strength, whether we accept or resist. We are called to carve out what we need, to speak up for ourselves, and to say no to what we don't want. At times, this can be terrifying, especially if our false self was based on pleasing others and keeping our needs hidden. It may mean making big changes in our lives and relationships.

> *I can give it to myself. Whatever I need, I can give. I no longer need to take, greedily and sneakily, from the wrong places. In my hunger, I no longer have to take. I can give. How I longed for rest, yet I couldn't lie down. How I longed for appreciation, and yet I went looking for it where it was least likely to be found.*

As I acclimatised to being with myself in this way, I came to appreciate the crucial importance of honesty. There is a deep integrity to this kind of honesty, a sense of being real that comes as a profound relief. It is not about attempting to tailor our experience to what we believe it should be, nor is it the spin of the persona trying to keep its narrative intact. What is actually here? What is most real in this moment? We discover a desire to become intimate with the realness of the moment, as Candace describes:

It's the realness of being, just being in contact with what's here. It doesn't depend so much on what the state is; it's the realness that seems to transmit. All I want is to be here in the realness.[46]

In the adapted, conditioned state, I had been starved of intimacy and connection. I was hungry for real contact with what had been locked away behind the defences. Even though making that contact was terrifying, it was also a relief. The deadness of the false began to give way to the aliveness of the real. Having been absent from myself in fundamental ways, I began to connect with and become present to my deepest, most hidden parts. I realised presence had always been present; it had known even my absence. Unendingly generous presence had held it all. The ultimate allowing, it even included absence. I had always been there, even when it felt like I wasn't. As time wore on, I began to feel more real, more embodied.

In our conversation, Andrew commented that it takes a while to understand the subtleties of being present, and that was also my experience. My capacity to be present developed as the dark night continued. I realised it was not a matter of trying to be present, that no effort was required simply to be here. As time went on, I became much more honest. It was not that I had been wilfully lying or denying reality before, but that now I was willing to be with whatever was truest in each moment. As my pretences faded, I was brought to my authentic self. I began to take the risk of being here. After all, I did not come here merely

---

[46] Candace, in conversation.

to observe, but to be in every thought, in each word, in every tear, in each smile; to act, feel, rage and move.

To all my fellow travellers: think your thoughts, feel your feelings; that's what they are here for. Don't stand back from your life. Marvel at your thoughts, at the miracle of imagining. Wonder at your feelings, the intimate play of emotion. Rejoice in your body's contortions, the aches of the flesh. Do yourself the favour of not pretending, except when you need to.

Chapter Seven: Finding the One We Lost

You are the untold depths into which you long to dive.

A deep yearning resided within me from a young age. Possessions and achievements could not fulfil this elemental longing, nor could the modest success I attained. Mostly the feeling was subliminal, a nagging sense of "This isn't it. There must be more to life than this," an emptiness or hollowness within. Every now and then, it felt like an unfillable chasm. It whispered or howled in the small hours when the busyness of life did not distract me. It attempted to bring my attention to what was missing, to what seemed lost.

For many years, I believed the resolution to this yearning lay in meeting the right person. A perennial desire for "the one" drove me into mismatched relationships hoisted by desperation, loneliness, and the hope that *this* time it would work. The idea of the perfect mate who would meet all my needs, a fairy-tale happy-ever-after, ran deep. Such fantasies soured as I met the reality of each relationship. Ultimately, I came to realise I would not find the perfect other I yearned for within another human being, although I am sure that true communion can bring it closer, as can connection with nature and creativity.

As the dark night wore on, I became immersed in the longing. I came to see that, contrary to what I had believed, the longing wasn't wrong. In fact, it was the truest thing here. I saw how the longing had become too much, had overwhelmed me and become fear, need and desire. My troubles had started when I turned away from the longing. A thousand sign posts had blocked my way home, all of them pointing in the wrong direction. Now I turned about-face and let the longing have me.

Once in a while, I found myself meeting what I longed for. It came in a variety of guises. The word *you* seemed to describe it best. At times, this *you* felt like my soul self, the real or essential self I thought I had lost. At other times, it felt like the divine in some shape or form, the sense of presence that infuses and animates life. Sometimes the word *God* felt apt. This was not at all about a belief in the god(s) or goddesses of religion; it was a direct sensing or knowing of something beyond my usual self with which I was deeply intimate and from which I was not at all separate. These glimpses—barely enough to keep me going through the long days of the dark night—felt like manna from heaven when I was otherwise starving.

The dark night was a process of retrieving what I perceived I had lost, and my grief for this loss was overpowering at times. It was profound, therefore, to realise that what I had been looking for had been patiently waiting for me, albeit out of sight and certainly out of mind. I had missed it so much. Without it, I had been completely bereft, totally devastated. I thought I had lost myself and the *you*. My searching had been so desperate that when I finally got to the *you*, I was beside myself:

I'm holding you, I won't let you go. Oh God, I've been terrified. I think this is what T. S. Eliot meant...[47] I'm coming back to myself. I'm coming home. It's me I've been trying to find all this time. It's me I've been looking for. This is what I had when I was little. I had my soul, and it was real, and I could see it all. But I was too little, and it was too much, and no one else could see it. And I've been terrified since I lost that connection.

This opening into my real self left me vulnerable, insecure and doubting. I was stripped of everything; the certainty of beliefs, ideas and constructs ebbed away. But even though the thought of being without the protection and familiarity of the persona was terrifying, I was even more terrified I had permanently lost the connection to my essential self. However much I doubted at times, there was nothing I desired more than to return to myself, to be reunited with what I had lost. Everything I had known and everything I had been taught was peeled away, layer by layer. In this terrain, I could not account for what I was perceiving within my normal terms of reference, yet I knew that this was what I had been waiting for.

Much as I yearned to reconnect with the *you*, I resisted its calling. I intuited that following its call would take me even further out of the known and familiar, so I vacillated and delayed for as long as I could. I pretended it wasn't here, like a child covering her eyes to trick herself into believing it didn't exist, when all the time it was in every step, in every word. I rationed it, as if it could be rationed. I denied it. I kept it to myself, not daring to share it. I acted as if it was not my all and everything. Not yet

---

[47] I had been reading T. S. Eliot's poem "Little Gidding."

willing to go all in, I thought I could ignore its call and thus preserve my sanctity. I had to go down every conceivable path to verify for myself that they were all dead ends. The panic intensified as I realised that every possible escape route was unviable. I was caught in an impasse; there was no way out. Having been brought to my knees, I began to listen. Thankfully, the call had continued regardless of my ignoring it. It had left clues for me, hinting at its presence in words, music, tears and mothering. It had kept vigil in the dark during the long, cold winter. It had survived on meagre rations and a few precious drops of water in drought conditions. It had never given up, despite my protestations and refusals, despite my declining its countless invitations.

I began hearing familiar ideas anew. Words I had previously read or been taught came into consciousness redolent with meaning. Having attended a nonconformist church as a child, I was well-versed in a tolerant, relatively inclusive version of Christianity. Although I had barely set foot in a church since the age of eighteen, biblical phrases started spontaneously coming to mind, an experience I initially found perplexing. The story of Jesus took on new connotations as an allegory of the dark night. Tempted in the wilderness by the pull of denial; praying in the garden of Gethsemane for reprieve; finally, being willing to prepare for Golgotha, to die to what he thought he was—all of it now made sense from an altogether different perspective. I barely mentioned this understanding to anyone for many years, scared of judgement or misinterpretation.

Forgive me, Father, for I know not what I do… I don't know who I am, if I can find all those parts of me again, to make myself one again, one with my soul.

Likewise, the words of the fourteenth-century Sufi poet Hafiz begun to have a strong resonance for me. His collection of words for the *you*, his delight, humour and tenderness, rang down the centuries, even through the lamina of translation. Of course, the mystical path does not belong to any one tradition, religion or culture, although our background informs our individual experience of it. Again, this is not a matter of taking on more beliefs or adding on identity. Rather, these are moments of gnosis. Our culture, language and individuality are the prisms through which the light of gnosis is refracted, giving it a specific hue.

As I began to glimpse the *you*, my trust in the process increased. Now I knew without doubt that my seeking was not mistaken or in vain. My persona could temporarily lay down its burden, a mercy after so much intense suffering. One day I found myself on my knees in worship. The *you* had stopped me from doing this before I was ready. I was so grateful to it. I bowed down before it. I gave my life to it. I asked it for forgiveness. It had always been there, and it had always loved me. Even though such moments left my mind reeling, and the words that came seemed incomprehensible to my intellect, they came nevertheless. My soul rejoiced. This was what I had been starving for.

Again, this reconnection with the *you* has nothing to do with codified spiritual or religious practices or concepts. The exact nature of the *you* is deeply mysterious and defies description. Yet when we are in touch with it, this sense of presence, our senses come alive. We know without doubt it is what we have been searching out or waiting for. We know it is home; we know it is that for which we have yearned. It is the most intimate part of our being, the essence of humanity and divinity. When we encounter it, we feel awe, gratitude and relief throughout our being, often accompanied by tears. The persona finds itself able to breathe again. Our encounters with the *you* tend to come when we are being most real, when we are feeling whatever is here in all its rawness. Like thirsty travellers coming upon an oasis, we have longed to immerse ourselves in these depths. We have awaited this baptism.

> *You waited for me. I thought you'd gone, and the pain was unimaginable. I was right, all this time. I didn't give up. Thank God I didn't give up. I thought I'd never find you. I thought I'd never get to you. I tried to forget you. I tried to go out there. But really, I just wanted to come back to you. I thought I wasn't you.*
>
> *I was so scared. I lost you once. I couldn't bear to lose you again. I knew you were here. I got myself to you in rags, on my hands and knees, utterly exhausted. I made it, limping and battle-weary, into your arms. I made it over the border, across the mountains at night. And you fed me, clothed me, took me in. You never left my side.*

One afternoon in the early days of my dark night, I met a moment from around the age of six. It was in that moment I had concluded I was ugly, or at least not pretty. Prior to that time, I had had no clear concept of beauty, prettiness or ugliness. As I felt the searing pain of that conviction,

I suddenly looked up through my tears and beauty was all I could see. Beauty was everywhere and everything, including me. It was not that I then became convinced of my beauty; no belief was replaced by its opposite. It was simply that for an hour or so, I experienced everything as beauty. It was as if my willingness to be with myself in that place had opened a crack through which the divine could enter. A voice of wisdom emerged that I could not claim as my own. I realised all my ideas about what is and is not beautiful or spiritual were moot; life itself makes no such distinctions. The temple may be profane and the market sacred; the *you* is everywhere, unbounded by buildings or beliefs.

There were many times during the dark night when I felt I was beyond redemption. I believed I was too flawed, broken, damaged or in pain ever to recover. I found myself with no option left but to pray, regardless of any ideas I had about what prayer was or even what or who I was praying to. These were the prayers of the desperate, besieged persona as it realised it could not continue on alone. Having finally realised it had isolated itself within its own now fatally breached defences, it had reached the point of surrender.

> *I am a very scared little girl. Oh God. I don't know what to do. Please help me. Please make it stop now. Please give me a way out of all this... I can't do this shit any more. Please show me who I am. What am I? None of it was true. I want to be someone else. All I have ever been is a rejection of me. There is nothing else left. Just show me, please. There is no more hope. There is no more future. I want to go home. Oh God, take me. I haven't got anything else.*

Even though she had never prayed before, Sophie also recalled praying during the worst two years of her dark night. She had moved to a new town just before the falling apart began.

> I remember lying in the bath praying. When I think back to that time, how hard it was, I just lay in the bath praying while every single thing around me fell apart. Everything absolutely fell apart. I'd be paralysed in the bathtub in this really tiny flat. And no one could understand it. I couldn't understand it. I couldn't explain it to anyone. It was absolutely horrendous.[48]

There is something deeply moving about such raw vulnerability, even as we are feeling it. The false self gives up its isolation and reaches out in supplication. Utterly humbled, it asks for help. Its brashness, hardness and harshness now almost entirely dissolved, the persona accepts that despite its best and valiant efforts, it cannot hold out any longer. Candace says:

> It's that "Please help me." It's that beautiful humility and vulnerability and emptiness, the emptiness of "Please help me." It's beautiful. It's like the opposite of the personal will.[49]

I continued to have out-of-the-blue moments of gnosis, prayer and surrender. Every time I connected with the *you*, the encounter subtly changed me. I could not un-know the other facets of reality that I now knew. My self-awareness increased. Having seen it from the perspective of

---

[48] Sophie, in conversation.
[49] Candace, in conversation.

the *you*, I became ever more conscious of the subtleties of my persona. Even though it had believed it had to do everything by itself, I realised that on this level of being, I had never been alone. The *you* had come with me. It hadn't left me or abandoned me. It had stayed with me, even when I couldn't see it, even as I was fighting it. It had held and loved me, whatever my embattled ego imagined. I had been looking for a love that had always been there and would always remain. Such peak moments sometimes resonated for days afterwards. On other occasions they unceremoniously vanished as the next wave of pain appeared.

Once I began to taste the *you*, I mourned even more deeply for the years of separation. I had missed my forgotten soul self. I began to understand—dimly at first, then with ever-increasing clarity—the tragedy of this disconnection. Grieving for this loss was absolutely necessary. I could no longer gloss over it or pretend it wasn't as it was. I knew what I had disconnected from, what I had lost. The numbness, dullness and disconnectedness had been there since I had been a child, reading cereal packets at the breakfast table in an attempt to shut out the discomfort within me and the atmosphere around me. I had separated myself at the deepest level. I had lost heart and had to survive in my head alone.

There had been a time before the disconnection, when it was okay to be myself, unadorned, unabashed, unabated. Something in me remembered how it was to be my real self. My realness, when I landed in it, was intoxicating and enlivening. I had thought I was supposed to be different. I had tried to stop myself from being Fiona. I had lost myself, even though I had tried not to. I hadn't known it was alright to be me. Now, I wanted to surrender to me, the absolute me-ness of me, the infinite love and patience of me.

Connecting with the *you*—or real me—in this way gave rise to awe and reverence. I tasted the immensity and miraculousness of existence. In those moments I felt included, loved and blessed. I had often doubted life's invitation was meant for me. I had assumed I was excluded or unworthy of an invite. Yet the same invitation issues forth to each of us in a multitude of ways. It is simply the invitation to recognise we are alive.

> *Tonight, my heart is breaking from the perfection of it all, from such translucent beauty. I felt I wasn't seen, yet your gaze never left me for a second. I thought I wasn't included, yet now I see you never, ever left me out. All of it—all of me—is so tenderly, delicately held. I didn't know where you'd gone. I had no idea you were everywhere, in everything, in every sight, in every sound, each breath, each smile, each exchange. How could I have ever been anything other than utterly innocent? How could any of us be? All of it—all of it—is such a miracle. Our sheer existence is such utter perfection. Let alone thoughts, music, trees, friends, rocks, beliefs and all the other myriad forms of creation, the ten thousand things.*

Such glimpses began to shape me. Having tasted sacredness, I now knew it had nothing to do with spiritual beliefs or any notion of being a spiritual person. In fact, my interest in using spirituality as a way to save myself waned to nothing. The more I connected with the *you*, the more evident it became that lost and found had never really been separate from each other.

It was a deep relief to stop looking, yet it was also clear the seeking had not been wrong in any way. It had brought me here, to the sacred.

After encounters with the *you*, I would sometimes feel even worse for a while. The structure of the persona would fight back, trying harder than ever to stay intact. Knowing its number was up, it would protest loudly, kicking and screaming. I felt as if I had taken a leap forward and then fallen back even further, as if I were losing a cosmic game of Snakes and Ladders. I would doubt the mystical occurrences, recasting them as some kind of wishful thinking or naivety. But the *you* persisted in many forms; it wasn't taking no for an answer. Gradually I began to accept that I was a child of this Hermetical world, for better or worse.

Reconnecting with the *you* was also profoundly validating. Despite my best efforts, I had never really felt adept at operating in the material world. Like the proverbial square peg, I did not comfortably fit the mould required to function within conventional society. I finally understood my struggle; some spark within me was more ethereal than corporeal. I was more at home in the intangible. Much as I had tried to be a successful someone, it had been a wrench. Having scorned sensitivity in others, I realised I had numbed and blunted my own. I remembered the unfettered sense of me I had as a young child, when I would unselfconsciously write, draw, colour, cut out and stick, all without injunctions or criticism. I began to play again.

Whatever your encounters with the *you*, know that they are genuine. Your experience may not fit anything you have read or heard anyone else describe, and it may go against your existing beliefs. In one moment I met an angelic presence, despite having derided the idea of their existence. Likewise, I had a powerful episode of communing with two souls from some other place, time or dimension. In their presence, I felt a love and connectedness I have rarely felt in this lifetime. I had missed them profoundly and had been awaiting their return. The joy of feeling seen and known by them in those moments was transcendent. Again, I had only ever flirted briefly with the idea of past or parallel lives, yet this experience happened nonetheless. The *you* makes itself known in an assortment of garbs, whatever our beliefs or lack thereof.

Each time I found the one I thought I had lost, boundless treasures became apparent. Seeing the miraculousness and magnificence of life happened in instants, yet the echoes of such moments resonated indefinitely. My needs and desires remained, as did my pain, but I was more tender with them now they had been illuminated by the glow of gnosis. It was a profound relief and privilege to stand unapologetically in the realness of my being. There was a standing down, a laying down of arms. It was clear I could not somehow use the sacred as a way to circumvent my travails. Indeed, the *you* demanded everything; the dark night is no half-measured devastation. Now I dwell in two dimensions, a foot in each. I am a flesh and blood creature, made for impermanence. And here in the silent sumptuousness of now, there is a realm of pristine, unadulterated newness, free of castles or fortresses. My soul insists I pay my dues to both above and below, body and psyche, land and sea.

Chapter Eight: Beginning to Trust

The development of the persona tends to result in a lack of trust. Turning away from our innermost being towards a mask necessitates overriding our instincts. I was aware of having overridden, overreached and overstretched myself countless times. I had come to mistrust my feelings and my judgement, which seemed undeniably faulty. I was unwilling or unable to access or act on my deeper knowing or gut reactions; my persona did not trust them. I looked elsewhere for guidance, answers and fulfilment. I held onto things that weren't okay for me because I doubted there would be anything else. My sense was that if I didn't cling to what I had, however ill-fitting it may be, I would have nothing. Time and again, this lack of trust took me to places I knew I should not go. During the dark night, I atoned for the years of mistrust and the ways in which I had consequently betrayed myself. Rachel describes how she lost any remaining shred of trust she had previously had in life:

> The biggest thing was, up until that time, there was still this trust that I'd had since I can remember that life always had your back. I'd always had that belief. And then, even that went. And it was "Fuck, I don't even trust that any more." That really shook me. There was nothing. My trust in trust had gone.[50]

---

[50] Rachel, in conversation.

In the depths of the dark night, I doubted myself to the core. I was stripped of self-confidence. Yet the mistrust eventually and inexorably gave way, and a new form of trust began to emerge, deeper and less conditional than the expectant trust of the persona. Even an occasional whisper of this trust carried me a long way. I fought and struggled, but I came to trust even the fighting and struggling. I developed an unforced commitment to and a trust in being with whatever was here. As this trust developed, it mattered less when what I was hearing from within was unfathomable, uncomfortable or inconvenient. I came to trust wherever life was leading me moment by moment. My perspective shifted from assuming something was wrong with my experience to a sense of "this too, even this." I began to feel a sense of readiness along with the trust.

> *I wasn't ready [to come home]. It all had to be given its due. It all had to be done: every step, each word. You have to be ready. When you're ready to accept the invitation, prepare for the journey. When there are words to be spoken, speak. Where there are tears to be shed, weep. When a view appears before you, look.*

Such trust is usually forged in solitude. When everything else has stopped working, when we find ourselves in a place of no hope and no help, we have no choice but to discover our inner resources, such as they are in each moment. When we are willing to jump, live or die, trust begins to emerge. When we have nothing left to hold onto, we discover what we can and cannot trust. We begin to trust both the process itself and our soul voice. Andrew says:

It's a kind of trust that comes when everything else is broken. You can't make a mood of the trust. It's not sincere until you really, really have no other … well, it's not even choice. It just happens. Innocence and trust don't come from any kind of effort.[51]

As trust in my inner promptings developed, I began to navigate the dark night a little more consciously. No doubt my eyes were also becoming accustomed to the dark. Once I was willing to trust the unerring guidance from within, I came to realise that no one else could possibly know where my path needed to take me. I began to look for companions and fellow travellers rather than teachers or authorities. When I recognised a movement towards or away from something, be it a person, book, teaching, activity, place or anything else, I learnt to go with it as best I could. There were many occasions when trusting this subtle, inner discernment felt awkward, crazy, silly or strange, but after a while, it became more natural. Daring to trust myself in this way was even liberating and exhilarating at times. I found myself doing and being in previously unthinkable ways, breaking out of orthodoxies and habits to which I had long subscribed. I became more adept at following each impetus as it came, at understanding the continued unfolding of the dark night even as I moved above ground part of the time. As I noticed what wanted to express in each moment, unexpected impulses sometimes arose. Candace describes her experience of finding her way:

---

[51] Andrew, in conversation.

You have to get on the bike and ride it. There's this impetus, a flow, and then I'll notice my mind will come in with old conditioning. I'll have these ideas of what it's supposed to look like, how to navigate… It's like an entirely new way, and it's about letting this impetus, this movement I feel in my body … Where is this going? What's the flow? How do I get on board with it? It's not like anybody's going to hand us a map. It's very uncharted ground.[52]

As my trust increased, the insistent comparing, measuring, evaluating and monitoring of myself that had been such a strong component of my persona gradually lessened. I would find myself in a variety of states with far less self-judgement or criticism. Even feeling shame evoked less shame. One evening, I spent a few hours in a state of grace. It felt as if love had taken everything out of my hands, robbing me blind and leaving me in stillness. Two days later, I connected with a trenchant sense of unforgiveness. Both seemed as real and valid as each other. I was as I was in each moment, come what may, without attempting to finesse or manipulate my experience.

Previously, I had used knowledge to shore myself up against life's unknowns, as if I could understand the mysteries of existence if I acquired sufficient information. I had to know. I had to know what had happened and what was going to happen. More than that, there was a sense that I should know, that I should have known. I thought I knew better. I thought I had to work it all out. Accruing knowledge had also been a way to protect

[52] Candace, in conversation.

myself from feeling; intellectual knowing had become a substitute for raw experiencing. Working out why I was feeling the way I did and being able to talk about cause and effect, however articulately, were poor substitutes for actually feeling what was going on in my body in all its messy, uncomfortable, painful, visceral truth. I had clung to the certainty of knowledge—even if it was of dubious validity—to avoid the uncertainty of the unknown. As I began to trust, I finally acknowledged the stunning extent of my not-knowing. I really didn't know anything. There was no way to ever know. The unknowing was complete, and I was humbled.

The act of trusting our real selves is inseparable from trusting our bodies. During the dark night, we begin to hear and understand the meanings and messages in sensations and symptoms rather than dismissing or silencing them. The body knows the truth of what has happened even as our minds might try to make the happened unhappen. As we begin to trust its expressions, its imagery and energy, we come to a profound appreciation for its intelligence, as Candace describes:

> It's really about trusting this intelligence that's in the body. I've had a particular contraction for a long time and I think it's very young. I've done a lot of work with it. Whenever I feel it tightening up, I just stop. I look in, get quiet, and let my body unwind.[53]

The greater our willingness to be with our bodies, the more unconditional our trust becomes. We become willing to be with our somatic

---

[53] Candace, in conversation.

experience—sensations, emotions, senses, movements and energies, along with the plethora of images and thoughts that accompany them. We let it all unfold in an organic, fluid way. The more we trust the natural unfolding of the process, the greater the depths we reach and the more insight we gain. We begin to honour how the process is evolving within us, rather than comparing ourselves to other people and concluding we are either less than or more than. Staying true to ourselves can be hard. We each experience a unique version of the dark night.

Trusting ourselves necessitates questioning and often rejecting what we have been taught. Our relationship to spirituality or religion is likely to undergo a profound change during this time. I can no longer partake of that which does not speak to my inner experience and knowing. Any philosophy that does not apprehend the paradoxical nature of life no longer makes sense. Any teaching that prefers positive to negative, light to dark, or the transcendent to the prosaic now feels like a violation. In my view, the ersatz spirituality of wish fulfilment infantilizes its believers. Being caught up in the game of guru and disciple can likewise keep us from realising our own authority and agency. Spiritual teachers who hawk disingenuous promises of permanent bliss are the contemporary version of the medieval indulgence sellers. I suspect most religious and spiritual codes only came into being because we lost our connection to the sacred. The sacred was separated from the worldly, for the profit and power of a small minority. Mature spirituality is unrelated to belief systems. It is simply the knowing of the sacred, both within ourselves and beyond. As I have said, it does not exclude the other aspects of our being; we all run the gamut from ridiculous to divine.

My sense is that much spiritual or religious practice is an attempt to recreate what spontaneously happens in moments when we find ourselves in a state of grace. In that state, it is natural to kneel in gratitude or awe, or to sit in silence, immersed in the intimacy of the present. We effortlessly wonder at the thrumming aliveness around and within us even as we are sitting on a bus or making dinner. It seems we presume that if we imitate such occurrences, we will reach a state of grace or peace. In a spiritual version of trying to fake it until we make it, we attempt to circumvent or get rid of any thoughts and feelings we believe should not be there. Thus the persona co-opts the notion of being spiritual as yet another way to avoid the pain it has been structured to avoid. Deeming ourselves "spiritual" may include the sense that we are better or more conscious than those we deem "unspiritual." During the dark night, the idea of spiritual practice or belief as a means to reach a predetermined destination becomes meaningless. We discover that if we stay with the truth of the moment, such as it is, we find ourselves dropping through to the numinous in unexpected ways:

> *The utmost gratitude for life, prostrate on the floor. Now I know why people kneel in prayer, the natural posture of gratitude. Utter, utter thankfulness, for all of it. Then I am overcome with love for all of it, every last thing. After a while, that turns to "I've come home." And a feeling that I thought I never would.*

The idea of enlightenment or awakening itself comes under scrutiny. It is natural for us to explore spirituality in the dark night, for what we are experiencing is soul-related. Much of what we find in the spiritual marketplace, however, promotes the fantasy of enlightenment as the ultimate escape from the reality of being human, yet another version of the quest to reach the ego ideal. It purports to offer a means to transcend our pain and discomfort, if only we think the right thoughts or undertake the right practices. We attempt to reach enlightenment—whatever our conception of it—by separating even further from ourselves and our bodies. Reading or listening to such material can compound our difficulties, especially when it intimates our suffering is somehow our own fault. For a short while, I fell prey to this trap in a big way, measuring myself with the enlightenment yardstick and coming up wanting. Awakening—or the idea of awakening—became another stick with which to beat myself, another milestone not yet achieved, another thing I had failed to understand or grasp. I believed that I wasn't good enough to get there, that my lack of enlightenment was proof positive of my irredeemable brokenness. Even though I had repeatedly glimpsed otherwise, the idea that happiness equals success and anything other than happiness equals failure persisted. I was ripe for the lure of enlightenment, a fantasy tailor-made for perfectionists with low self-esteem.

Such transcendent, upwards-and-outwards spirituality is directly at odds with the natural movement of the dark night. Trying to escape by espousing what Luann calls "rocket ship spirituality" is ultimately doomed to failure, partly because it is exhausting and partly because it is a lie:

> The rocket ship spirituality—one of the survival instincts was to try to stay up here, but it was so much effort to keep my thoughts and actions and so forth in that spiritual place. That too was exhausting, so that rocket ship to spirituality wasn't sustainable. It felt good to be up there, but it didn't feel correct or right, because it was so hard to stay up there.[54]

The notion that we can bypass the reality of our pain is a kind of violence. In fact, the idea that life should be free from pain begins to seem bizarre. We become radically honest, no longer willing to dissemble or hide, at least from ourselves. Knowing the richness and depth of ourselves, we can no longer countenance excluding, discounting, denying or demonising any aspect of our being. We begin to distinguish between the fantasy of awakening and the reality of our experience, however mundane or sublime it is in each moment. We develop greater discernment in relation to spiritual teachings and offerings, having the nous to distinguish between what is or is not conducive to our unfolding.

Likewise, the prevalent notion that we should indiscriminately accept, forgive, or surrender becomes anathematic. Attempting to accept the unacceptable or forgive the unforgivable involves contorting and distorting ourselves into denying the reality of our experience. The more we trust the process, the more we realise the equal validity of acceptance

---

[54] Luann, in conversation.

and non-acceptance, forgiveness and unforgiveness, and surrender and resistance. Forgiveness, acceptance or surrender come on their own terms and in their own time, not because we have willed them. When they come of their own volition, we taste their inimitable sweetness. Having frequently castigated myself for poor relationship choices, forgiveness came flooding in one day.

> *I can start again. I can be reborn. It is all forgiven. I thought I wasn't forgiven. I forgive myself. I forgive myself for being with the wrong people in the wrong places. I forgive myself for my desperation, my loneliness and my pain. I forgive myself for needing love, warmth and company. I forgive myself for being insecure, and for giving away parts of myself in an attempt to find love. I understand now, and I forgive myself.*

Insights into the nature of ourselves and life come aplenty. Such insights have nothing to do with ideas or concepts but are a seeing and knowing within our whole being. As each insight comes, we experience it fully for as long as it is alive within us. Once gone, we do not attempt to fossilize it or recast it as a rule or inviolable truth. We know the reality of paradox and polarity. One day, as I was walking into the local supermarket, I suddenly realised there is ultimately no right or wrong. It was a profoundly moving moment. For a few hours, I saw both myself and everyone else through this beyond-right-or-wrong lens. Afterwards, my sense of right and wrong was even clearer than it had ever been. No longer holding on to spiritual concepts or aphorisms as if they were buoyancy aids, we are willing to risk plunging into the choppy waters of direct, unfiltered experience.

Sometimes the realisations that come make no logical sense. They certainly do not conform to our existing beliefs or conceptual frameworks. We suddenly perceive reality from an entirely different perspective. Such rarefied realisations do not render our normal perception or perspectives faulty in any way because the two coexist; in those moments, we are simply seeing from another vantage point. We do not retrospectively need to make sense of what we have perceived, for in the moment there is complete, if inexpressible, understanding.

> *There's nothing but me. I thought there were different things, good things and bad things. There's me, trying to change the picture as if it contained anything other than me. All of it arising together: birth and death, beginning and ending, up and down, right and wrong, me and you; all of it so utterly okay. All resistance melts away.*
>
> *I thought there was this thing called presence that I didn't have (that's really funny). It's all included in the price. Nothing gets left behind. And nothing needs to get packed away or disposed of or boxed up. Nothing is excluded or deemed unacceptable. We deny our total acceptability, believing ourselves unworthy, deeply flawed, or incomplete, but we've already been given our boarding pass. Stunned, one day we discover there is nothing to reject, and no exclusions, no caveats, no conditions.*

As I began to trust my inner experience more fully, my life deepened, a deepening that seemingly has no end. I became a bit more stable, or perhaps more used to instability, even though the swings of the pendulum were still considerable. Having been in the *yin* underworld for so long, *yin* and *yang* started to balance a little more. I moved with more fluidity between open and closed, outer and inner, doing and idleness, light and dark, up and down. I discovered that the reality of awakening bore no relation to the bliss-and-peace-filled fantasies I had come across. This undoing left me with no place to land and nothing to hold onto. The dark night slaughters all our sacred cows, and the slaughter doesn't stop.

Chapter Nine: Emerging

These are the ashes, and maybe somewhere in here there's a phoenix.

The language of alchemy arose throughout my dark night. Alchemising is an arduous and rigorous procedure involving a number of stages, each with its own quality. First came the phases of dissolution, when it seemed as if the weeping would never cease. I was broken down into fragments. I underwent a process akin to purification, the real within me being distilled from the false. I was fermented in the crucible of darkness. And eventually it was time for the burning. I found myself willing to go to the flames. Finally I was all in, ready to be consumed by the fire. I had wanted to say yes but hadn't known how until I found myself on the pyre. I had thought safety lay in saying no, but I was wrong. In saying yes, I saw the sacredness of life, the miraculousness that had been waiting for me all along. All of it, including my exquisite singularity, was given to me to marvel at.

Once I said yes, I could not do, manage or contain the process— it was happening regardless of my interventions or otherwise. I became less frantic. All I did was commit to being present as best I could, as messily as I did. The distillation continued at its own pace, with its own intelligence and logic, especially when I was still for a while. I was being undone. I could not possibly know how things should proceed or what should come next.

Put another way, I became willing to carry my own cross, for the persona to die so my real self could be resurrected. This period of crucifixion was excruciatingly painful, but I had come to desire it more than anything else. I found myself surrendered to the reality of whatever was here in each moment. This surrender did not render me passive; it brought me into the essence of my aliveness again and again. It was followed by a resurrection or ascension of sorts. Having come down and into my deepest self, I now began to unfurl very slowly outwards. Gradually, over the years, I found myself surrounded by the ashes of my former self and life, all of it consumed in the alembic of the dark night. Having been razed to the ground, I wondered how and where I could possibly go from here.

As I became more closely aligned with the real, I recognised the natural risings and fallings within, becoming ever more attuned to the currents. The drive to become more or less of anything—even to be more conscious or present—ebbed away as I realised I was present, full stop. I was here, even though part of me had been doing its best not to be. At first, the immediacy and directness of being here sometimes made me feel a bit nauseous. The sheer, unadulterated here-ness of here was breathtaking. There were so many stimuli. No wonder I had sought distractions with which to dilute life.

Whatever the circumstances of my outer life—and there have been profound challenges in recent years that have severely tested the mettle that was borne of the dark night—my inner life became simpler and continues to simplify. I discovered just being here was enough. yet I was not devoid of inspiration, motivation or direction. I wanted to be left to be me, unquestioned and untrammelled, yet I could respond and react as I needed to. Finally, I could just be. I unravelled and didn't unravel. I changed and stayed the same. It took a long time to get here, but it seems all of it had to happen—every last word, look, action—just as it did. The dark night began with the sudden, liberating sense that I could just be me. This coming back to myself continued, over and over again, with less fanfare each time.

Like me, Per began to emerge haltingly, shaking the ash from his feathers as he felt his way:

> How did I emerge out of it? Not by anything that I did. There was a turning point. The one thing I did—and I don't know if there's any causality there—I did an all-inclusive gratitude practice. I'd say, "I'm grateful for" and include everything. I did that every day for a few months, and somehow something shifted around that time and things started to feel lighter. There's still a lot of trauma to work on, but the intensity is not at all like it was. Things keep falling apart, but not the way they used to. Now things fall apart, and they come back together again.[55]

The dark night left me with a severe lack of confidence. Having lost my old identity, it took time to regain my self-esteem. I doubted and questioned myself. Having been humbled again and again, I felt like an

---

[55] Per, in conversation.

absolute beginner, building from scratch. I eventually left the relationship that had begun a few months prior to the crash and began to piece together a different kind of life. Leaving felt like a leap into the void. At the time I had virtually no income. But taking that leap galvanised me. I moved into a dilapidated house that needed a complete overhaul—the obvious symbolism of the move was not lost on me. It was disconcerting to edge out into the world again, having been cloistered for so long. It took time to learn how to navigate above ground.

I began very slowly, taking on a small amount of writing and editing work. A few months later, I found an ideally undemanding part-time job. At the time, I doubted my capacity to handle even that, but over the months it became easier. As I emerged, I needed time and stillness in which to digest everything that had happened in the underworld, to integrate and assimilate all that had occurred. I could not fashion a new life according to some predetermined plan. Rather, life evolved out of the remains of the dark night. Rachel describes her transition:

> The dark night was scary because I wondered if that was how it was going to be forever. It went on and on and on. Just when I thought there was a bit of space, there'd be more that needed to come out. I felt like I was really being squeezed. Every drop of these patterns and beliefs was wrung out of me. It's only these last three months that I feel like that has stopped. I've gone into this stillness, this sense of the space between no longer and not yet, this liminal space of integration and stillness where there's no longer a falling apart but there are no real fruits of that time yet to see.

I feel like a butterfly in the chrysalis. Now in the cocoon is this integration. There is nothing that can be done until it can be done. I've had to embody that. There is much more of a relaxation. There's no rush. What are we rushing to? People would say, "So what's your plan?" And I'd say, "I'm just here today right now." I've tried to plan. It doesn't come out like the plan at all. You can only do what you can do, so just do that. And that is enough. In fact, it's more than enough. Let go of the rest.[56]

Once in the ascent, the cycles of rising and falling continue. This is the ungainly stumbling of a newborn foal, not some glorious ascension into a hallowed future. The lessons from the dark night remain very much alive, and its reverberations continue. It has no definite end, as Sophie makes clear:

Nine years on, the process is still happening in me. I'm aware its work is not finished. I'm not going to be spat out and able to go back to my career. I feel like I'm being so utterly rewired still. It's ongoing in me. There's been some degree of reprieve, but it doesn't stop. It doesn't feel necessarily like it ever has a destination. Everyone's experience is so unique.[57]

Even though the unravelling continues, we have a greater capacity to be with ourselves, so our experiences become more tolerable. As Andrew says:

---

[56] Rachel, in conversation.
[57] Sophie, in conversation.

I don't think it really stops. It's just that we get better at handling it. And more aware of what's going on. And we have friends who can support us and understand. In a sense, things get harder and they get easier. They get easier because you're more skilled, and they get harder because you're dealing with deeper issues that are closer to the heart, the really dense knots that take a long time to deal with. I know people who still get thrown around tremendously, but it's more like water off a duck's back. It doesn't go as deep. There's some part of you that isn't touched by it.[58]

As I emerged, there were moments of laughter amidst the anguish and intensity and times when the density of the feelings gave rise to tears of laughter as well as pain. The process became less dramatic and all-consuming, and the paradoxes inherent in life and within myself became ever more evident. Absurdity and tragedy coexisted more comfortably when I could be with both. From a particular perspective, I could see an immense humour in the comedy of errors I had endured. There were moments when I got the cosmic joke, when the divine punchline finally made sense. As Candace shares:

I was laughing this morning in the midst of feeling this pushing up again and thinking how absurd it is that we walk ourselves to our own demise. Why would I do that? That's what we're doing. I think that's where the laughter comes from. It seems like I willingly did this.[59]

---

[58] Andrew, in conversation.
[59] Candace, in conversation.

My inner dialogue gradually morphed into a sometimes playful exchange, a far cry from the self-scorning I had previously endured. The harsh voice of my superego, which had seemed hell-bent on judging and second-guessing me, seemed to have gone quiet. The layer of thought whose job it was to comment on thoughts was no more. In its place was a wry, playful commentator who often dispensed truth with a glint of humour:

> *"Why not be happy?" I ask. "Because bad things happened," you reply. "People got hurt. I'm in pain. So I have no right to be happy." "I'm sorry," I say, "but all your objections are spectacularly beside the point. You can dance that dance if you want to, forever moving to the tunes of the past. There is an alternative, if you dare, but it does involve chucking yourself on the funeral pyre."*

Having faced the mystery of death, it was now time to confront the immensity of life. I began to let in the breathtaking enormity of my humanity. No longer constantly defending against life or my own vulnerability, I found myself encountering a quality of grace or mercy, a deep sense of love, compassion and kindness way beyond my personal understanding or capacity. I recognised this quality yet had often pretended I didn't because I feared both its vastness and simplicity. As Terry explains, I knew my experiencing of it was not personal. It did not make me special or unusual in any way:

> Why I'm in so much of a better place, why I'm able to enjoy my life now, is because these qualities of wisdom and oceanic compassion and mountainous strength are mine, but they're not

me. They're mine in as much as God or whatever makes them available to me. It's the difference between me the separate person who somehow is one day going to become a superhero—which hasn't happened yet—or the one who has given up being separate. And in giving up being separate, I noticed, "Oh Lord, all the stuff I was trying to get as a separate person is already here."[60]

This quality of grace or love left me with nothing yet felt like the greatest gift. A gentle love, it would steal upon me unexpectedly. At times, it felt too overwhelming, too spacious, too heartbreaking, yet I found myself giving over to it anyway. Unexpected moments of spontaneous awe and gratitude for the simplest of things welled up. Candace talks about this:

When I was really in that dark night, it was like holding on for dear life. It was an anguished cry, "I'm dying here." This has a very different quality, although there are similarities. It has a lot more vulnerability and innocence. Dark night felt like a death, really holding on and really dying. This feels like expanding. It doesn't feel so much like dying. It feels like being born again. When I stop, I've noticed this opens up into weeping. I tried to describe it to someone one day and I couldn't even really put a word to it. I'm being wept.[61]

One morning, I had a memory of myself at the age of ten, when I was on the cusp of losing contact with myself. Having loved writing from a young age, I was sitting at the dining room table working on an adaptation of

---

[60] Terry, in conversation.
[61] Candace, in conversation.

Romeo and Juliet. Very soon after that, my unbridled creativity shut down and I became painfully self-conscious. For the next forty years, I kept my writing hidden within my journals. Not long after this potent recollection I started a blog, words flowing again. I began to fit back into myself, remembering who I had been before I became adapted. Less hidebound by convention or conditioning, I became more profoundly individuated.

I retraced my steps back to old loves and interests, remembering what had delighted me as a child. I returned to the places where I had been shamed and reclaimed my talents. I began to accept my introversion, shyness and timidity rather than viewing them as flaws or faults to be corrected. I felt freer, wilder, more alive, less solid, more tentative. Having been anaesthetised for far too long, I was returning to consciousness. I realised I did not want to be tame. I had been tamed and had tried to stay tame, without success. Finally I had escaped to these wilder shores, no longer corralled, my heart singing songs of praise.

Slowly, I became more resourced to meet whatever arose. It was as if, by accompanying myself through the dark night, I aligned or connected with an aliveness and creativity far greater than my own. The realer I became, the more my resources grew. Now spending less of my energy on maintaining the structures of the adapted self, I was freer to create, to take the risk of being myself. Finally willing to get on the ride, I could make bigger gestures. I could stand, unapologetically. I could risk being seen.

This is not to say by any means that I did not or do not continue to come up against my conditioning or woundedness. There are many times when I find myself in that same blueprint. This is not about arriving in some fantastical Shangri-La where suffering is no more and we live an enchanted storybook life. Very little has changed in the geography of my life. I live in the same area, see many of the same friends, and love the same music. The difference is that I no longer mistake the skewed perception of the adapted self for reality. There are times when that skewed perspective feels like reality, but I know it is not, despite appearances. I have the means to be with and look deeply into whatever it is purporting to be the case. As a consequence, I am far less prone to acting out or creating drama.

Emerging from the dark night was akin to a process of coming out, a revelation of who I really am, body and soul. I was becoming what and who I had always been. I stopped delaying or denying the reality of myself. Emboldened, I began to embody and speak the unique truths of my existence, loudly or quietly. I stood up for and stepped into my realness, such as it was in each moment. The prevarication stopped and I committed fully to the unfolding. It became my all and everything. Candace says:

> It's the commitment, right? Not like I really believe we have a choice, but there is this "yes" that happens internally. It comes with tears, and with a lot of reckoning inside somehow, that I'm giving everything to this. It's not a hobby. It's not a belief system. It's everything.[62]

---

[62] Candace, in conversation.

Once I was committed, the ideas I had about my insufficiency or brokenness continued to fall away. One day I saw that there had never been anything wrong with me, an insight in stark contrast to my firm conviction of my inherent wrongness. Never anything wrong with what I said, how I felt, what I looked like, what I did, what I thought, or what my body did. The remnants of my adapted self sometimes freaked out when such revelations came. Deficiency was its forte, so this process was deeply challenging. Its ability to control how I appeared and what I was doing and saying gradually waned. At the same time, I came to appreciate it and all its quirks, foibles and neuroses, more and more.

As the adapted self lost momentum, I became more closely attuned to reality rather than to my fantasies, fears and delusions. This reattunement came about partly through profound real-time explorations of the fantasies, fears or delusions as they surfaced, rather than from resisting or dismissing them. I still explore in this way. The fluid inquiry that accidentally arose in the dark night has since been finely honed. There is beauty and relief in coming squarely back to reality, whatever its particular nature in the moment. The spontaneous perceptual shifts that happen through inquiry reveal the real in both its singularity and multiplicity, the one and the many. The marvels of existence become ever more apparent, yet life feels more normal, as do I. A union of individuality and life itself happens, and a deep integration takes place, as Candace describes:

This meeting is love. It's like the meeting of heaven and earth, the divine and the embodied, the animal nature. There's this love. And it is beautiful. Sometimes I just feel this surge of compassion for all of us who are in the various stages of this.[63]

There is an unfathomable stillness in this meeting place. The stillness has always been here, but we become much more conscious of it as time goes on. It is the stillness of sunrise and snowfall, the stillness implicit in being, the stillness that draws us to the earth. It carries a sense of the ancient. Women and men throughout the centuries have connected with it. Mountains, oceans, plains, trees; this ancient being or knowing knows and is known by us. When we feel it, we recognise we have missed it. We connect to the ancient within us and hold fast to it, come what may. This is the *you* in another guise. Anja describes her experience of it:

For the last months there are these intense storms, but I always come back here. It's a kind of wisdom, a knowing. The real holiday is the stillness. That changes everything. It's like a giving up, but not how the mind imagines giving up. It's a readiness, a kind of sweet surrender. There's a sweet sadness to it. This is love.[64]

Along with the storms and the stillness, I started to experience occasional moments of joy, often for no discernible reason. Such moments felt especially potent after long periods of anguish and distress. I was rising

---

[63] Candace, in conversation.
[64] Anja, in conversation.

from the ashes and coming back to life. Luann was driving down a mountain when she reconnected with her love of music, and hence life:

> There was one moment. I remember just having the thought pop into my head, "How do I get back to the piano?" Then it occurred to me, "I don't just want to play again. I want to love it again, like I did before." And then a few seconds later, it occurred to me, "Oh, I want to love life again." So that was huge, because then that told me, "Oh, I have a life." When those things started happening, it marked the beginning of the ascent. I could realise, "That's what all of this was for. I see."[65]

My rekindled love of life took on new and varied hues. Sometimes, I touched a love so vast it took me apart, slaying me to the core. It was the love spoken of in scriptures, tales and songs. Before the dark night, I had believed I had to hold myself back from love. I thought love was hurt and pain and would break me. I rarely loved unreservedly. I liked but did not all-out love. I was fond of, lusted after, and got on with, but only fleetingly loved without condition. Now, I found myself loving wholeheartedly. The objects or recipients of my love didn't seem so significant. It was the loving itself, a flight into total vulnerability, the giving of myself in this way. I began sharing my heart with whomever it resonated. To my delight, I found there were others like me. I wanted to love and be loved crazily and fearlessly. I wanted to drown in the *you*:

---

[65] Luann, in conversation.

The Dark Night of the Soul

Arms outstretched, hands in supplication: the gentle descent, the giving up. I'd missed the sheer heartbreaking, breathtaking, stunning beauty of life. It's all already here, freely given, no effort required. I thought there was something I had to do. I thought I had to earn it. I thought I had to be deserving. I thought love was conditional, depending on me earning or deserving it. I thought I wasn't loved. Simply a case of mistaking everything for nothing. I couldn't believe I'm loved this much.

Gradually, I found some strength amidst the ruins of my persona. Tempered in the forge of the dark night, my resolute commitment to meet the truth of my experience remained. My allegiance shifted from appearance to reality. I became braver. No longer content with half measures, I stopped compromising what was most important to me. Having endured the powerlessness and choicelessness of the dark night, I experienced a sense of agency once more. Unlike the coarser will of the adapted self, this sense of agency felt like an instinctual, uncomplicated movement towards or away from, a natural discernment. With minimal drama, I found myself moving towards or away from people, places, activities. Likewise, I felt a greater sense of agency in relation to my inner experience. No longer at the mercy of totally overwhelming emotions or forces, I behaved with greater maturity. As I continued to be with myself, particularly when unconscious patterns emerged, I became less neurotic and more capable and grounded. Having become more integrated, I acted with greater integrity. None of this was a matter of personal achievement, but a natural corollary of having been through the dark night, just as Candace describes:

When I was in the dark night, I remember periods on the couch, in my bed, on the floor, sobbing. I just couldn't move. This isn't like that. It's more energised and has a different quality. I didn't have so much strength in the dark night. It was like totally giving way. This is calling forth a strength in me.[66]

Having lost so much of what I had valued at the start of the dark night, I now discovered value in unexpected places, not least within me. I started to notice the undersides of life, seeing what had previously seemed insignificant or worthless. I remembered how tender I had been with everything when I was very young. Back then I had known it was all precious, that everything from specks of dirt to nuggets of gold had equal value. Until I forgot, succumbing to the belief that value is variable, that riches have greater intrinsic value than the lowliest of objects. Value has nothing, I repeat nothing, to do with economic worth, title or status. It cannot be earned or lost. Rather, it is measured in how closely we listen to the earth and to life's subtle whispers, in how gently we touch the lowest of the lowlies. I saw that we are here to care for things, to be custodians. I remembered the language of the heart that I had known so long ago.

In the glow of the dark night's embers, I began to revel in living itself, in the sheer aliveness of life. How had I missed this for so long, this incredible, beautiful, heartbreaking, soaring, funny aliveness? How could I not put "Oh my God" at the end of every sentence, every sight and sound? Yet I had pretended to ignore the magnificence and the mystery. I had had

---

[66] Candace, in conversation.

the chutzpah to pretend I knew what was going on when in reality I didn't have the slightest idea. When I finally admitted that, life became richer, deeper, fuller. My cup ran over. Having been cautious, held back, trouble-avoiding, safety-craving, I now wanted to hurl myself at life with reckless abandon. To dive into the mire and mess, wild and crazed, bloodied, dirty, dishevelled and fucked up. No more holding back, no more mincing words. Winds are not meek, and rain does not attempt to be less wet. Frost spares nothing, and the sun does not dim its own brightness. I was finally willing to be hurt, scarred, pierced or burnt to ash over and over again. I was finally willing to live.

Afterword

I often marvel at how my dark night turned out, how being in that place of excruciating anguish, untold terror and immense pain brought me so much. When it began, I could not imagine surviving it, let alone thriving again, but it was the making of me in ways I could never have foretold in the bleakest days and nights. Irrevocably changed by all that transpired, my life has become a testament to the never-ending unfolding that began during those years. Everyone I had conversations with in preparation for writing this book also expressed immense gratitude for the experience. Life tore us asunder so we could find what we had lost. The dark night took us into the most intense suffering we have ever endured, yet in retrospect we would not have missed a minute of it. We wouldn't wish it on anybody yet are unequivocally grateful to have gone through it, as Candace expresses:

> Standing in this place, looking back at all we've gone through, knowing what I know now, would I still say yes to this? Absolutely, yes.[67]

The dark night bestows rich insights into the human condition. It teaches what cannot be taught. Having come to know my inner landscape so thoroughly, I now commune with others as they journey through their own terrain. Individually and collectively, we are immersed in the rawness and reality of life. At least partially restored to our authenticity, we now have

---

[67] Candace, in conversation.

the fibre to be with the full spectrum of our experience. Our emotional resilience has increased, not because we are inured to our feelings, but because we are better equipped to be with them. Naturally, we still resist or rail against life at times. No longer trapped within the narrow confines of the adapted self, we can be in it all, denying nothing. We are as we are in any given moment without trying to escape, even when we are trying to escape. Living in this paradoxical, unconditional world is by turns heartbreaking, sane, startling, humdrum, painful, fulfilling and funny.

As the dark night wore on, it was as if I lost my persona's operating instructions. Without the manual on how to be Fiona, I could not come at life with a game plan. Slightly disconcerted yet profoundly relieved, I realised the dark night was just the start of a much bigger process. Life began to twist and turn in ways formerly unthinkable, and still does. As I wake from the trance of the persona and its habituated grooves of belief, assumption and consumption, I find myself less sharply defined by my history. The layers of false identity that shrouded my realness gradually peel away now I am willing to meet pain as it surfaces. I have reverted to my old self, to being the person I was born to be. It is mostly a delight to savour my original temperament free of the burdens it previously shouldered.

The dark night journey is completely countercultural. It passes largely unrecognised and unsupported, not least because it goes against society's grain. Yet the world itself appears to be in the throes of a dark night. The old structures, now demonstrably rotten, are falling apart. The nakedness of the emperors and their courtiers has been exposed, despite their desperate attempts to persuade us of the finery of their clothing. We do not yet know what will come in their stead; it sometimes feels as if the world is on the brink. Dismayed at what we are witnessing, we wonder what part we might play in this greater scheme of things. It is not that we have to be out in the world making big, bold statements; even the seemingly smallest and least significant of our actions has an effect. Life is calling us forth in a host of ways—to speak when we have been silent, be silent when we have spoken, create, act, move, be still. We cannot know what our part is until we find ourselves playing it. The call will persist, however deep our discomfort runs and however much we delay our response.

The dark night is a process of disillusionment, a bonfire of all our vanities. The burning, once begun, is ruthless. Any delusions we have about who we are or what we can claim for ourselves are scorched. Knowing we are neither superior nor inferior to anyone else, we become both more unassuming and more dignified. We have the fortitude to stand up for ourselves, to hold the line when it needs to be held. We can no longer be talked out of the truth of our experience. We discover a quiet authority within, a mature and common sense that can perceive and discern with clarity. While dramatic events may occur, we tend not to dramatize or overcomplicate what is happening in the ways we once did. On any given day, the simple act of being present without artifice or agenda can take us in any direction. We are willing to go wherever we are taken.

Wherever you are in your dark night journey, take heart. This is an invitation to come as you are. Commit to authenticity, to truth. Actually, even that is saying way too much. All you need do is be here, and love will do the rest. Listen to the sweet song of here. Drown in here. And know this: you are not alone. You are one of many who have trodden this path. Living or dead, near or far, we are your *anam cara*. When you are struggling to stand, you have our support. When you cannot take any more, you are in our hearts. We hear your prayers of desperation. We are with you in tears and laughter, in hope and resistance, in anguish and peace. You will come through this, because we did. This is the journey from absence to presence. You will find your way back to the heart of yourself.

Acknowledgements

I am immensely grateful to Per, Andrew, Sutra Ray, Rachel, Anja, Luann, Sophie, Stefano, Candace and Terry for sharing their experiences so openly and generously. My heartfelt thanks go to Stefan Armoneit for our conversations and his stunning cover art, and Claire Crevey for her sensitive editing and fabulous cover design. Thanks also to my trio of proof-readers —Amanda Tatton, Stephanie Robertson and Alex Mawson-Harris—who have gone above and beyond. Lastly, this book would not have been written without my own *anam cara*, my beloved fellow travellers. My endless gratitude to you all.

About the Author

Fiona Robertson is a facilitator and teacher of embodied inquiry who has been exploring the mystical realm for many years. She journeys with people— many of whom are going through or have experienced a dark night of the soul—into their interior landscape, accompanying them as they discover light where there was dark, dark where there was light, and often something entirely different on the other side. A creative and perceptive soul friend, she supports people from around the world to reconnect with and deepen into their real selves. She is the author of *The Art of Finding Yourself: Live Bravely and Awaken to your True Nature*, a collection of articles about the Living Inquiries. She loves acting, is an occasional poet, and lives in Nottingham, UK.

thedarknightofthesoul.com/
facebook.com/fionarobertsonauthor/

Printed in Great Britain
by Amazon